Vegetation Community Monitoring at Timucuan Ecological and Historic Preserve and Fort Caroline National Memorial, 2009

Natural Resource Data Series NPS/SECN/NRDS—2012/249

Michael W. Byrne and Sarah L. Corbett

USDI National Park Service
Southeast Coast Inventory and Monitoring Network
Cumberland Island National Seashore
101 Wheeler Street
Saint Marys, Georgia, 31558

and

Joseph C. DeVivo

USDI National Park Service
Southeast Coast Inventory and Monitoring Network
University of Georgia
160 Phoenix Road, Phillips Lab
Athens, Georgia, 30605

February 2012

U.S. Department of the Interior
National Park Service
Natural Resource Stewardship and Science
Fort Collins, Colorado

The National Park Service, Natural Resource Stewardship and Science office in Fort Collins, Colorado publishes a range of reports that address natural resource topics of interest and applicability to a broad audience in the National Park Service and others in natural resource management, including scientists, conservation and environmental constituencies, and the public.

The Natural Resource Data Series is intended for the timely release of basic data sets and data summaries. Care has been taken to assure accuracy of raw data values, but a thorough analysis and interpretation of the data has not been completed. Consequently, the initial analyses of data in this report are provisional and subject to change.

All manuscripts in the series receive the appropriate level of peer review to ensure that the information is scientifically credible, technically accurate, appropriately written for the intended audience, and designed and published in a professional manner.

This report received informal peer review by subject-matter experts who were not directly involved in the collection, analysis, or reporting of the data.

Data in this report were collected and analyzed using methods based on established, peer-reviewed protocols and were analyzed and interpreted within the guidelines of the protocols.

Views, statements, findings, conclusions, recommendations, and data in this report do not necessarily reflect views and policies of the National Park Service, U.S. Department of the Interior. Mention of trade names or commercial products does not constitute endorsement or recommendation for use by the U.S. Government.

This report is available from (http://science.nature.nps.gov/im/units/secn) and the Natural Resource Publications Management website (http://www.nature.nps.gov/publications/nrpm/).

Please cite this publication as:

NPS 006/112888, 396/112888, February 2012

Contents

Figures

Tables

List of Terms

Absolute cover: The total amount of ground surface that is covered by each species or group. Describes the amount of cover that each species or group represents in a stratum. Expressed as a percentage. Can exceed 100% due to overlap. The total cover of each species or group divided by the total possible cover for a plot.

Canopy species: Woody species known to occur in the midstory or overstory of the canopy, or shrub species that grow greater than or equal to 4 cm DBH and measureable at breast height (1.4 m).

Canopy stratum: The structural zone above 1.1 m (i.e., elbow height of a typical observer as per densiometer instructions) and consists of all live and dead plant material that affects the amount of light penetrating to the ground. This includes individual elements whose cover is also potentially measured and accounted for in the shrub- or groundcover-stratum measurements, but exceeds 1.1 m in height, is detected by the densiometer, and contributes to canopy cover. Also referred to as the midstory, overstory, or sub-canopy.

Cover: The vertical projection of the outermost extent of a species, or the extent of the shadow cast by the species if the sun were directly overhead. Foliar cover.

DBH: Diameter at breast height, or 1.4 m above the ground's surface.

Frequency: The number of times a species or group is detected in a plot, expressed as a percentage. Provides information on regularity at which a species or group is encountered.

Groundcover stratum: The structural zone that consists of all non-woody species (i.e., forbs and graminoids), and all woody species (i.e., shrubs and trees) with a DBH of less than 1 cm and seedlings 30 cm or less in height.

Relative cover: The cover of each species or group as a function of all other plant species that occurred in a plot. Describes the percentage of cover that each species represents out of the total vegetative cover in a stratum. Expressed as a percentage. Always sums to 100%. The total cover of each species or group divided by the sum of the cover of all other species that occur in a plot.

Seedlings: Woody dicotyledonous plants less than 30 cm in height.

Shrub stratum: All woody species greater than 30 cm in height with a DBH of 1–4 cm.

Stratum: A structural size category of vegetation at a site. These are the canopy, shrub, and groundcover layers.

Executive Summary

In 2009, the National Park Service (NPS) Southeast Coast Network (SECN) Inventory and Monitoring Network began collecting vegetation community data as part the NPS Vital Signs monitoring program. Information collected under this Vital Sign will be used to help managers make better informed decisions by understanding trends and variability related to plant species, frequency of occurrence, percent cover, diversity, and distribution in the groundcover, shrub, and canopy strata.

Within each stratum, vegetation communities were sampled using a hybrid of methods used by the North Carolina Vegetation Survey nested-subplot design (Peet et al. 1998) within a circular plot similar to the Forest Inventory and Analysis protocol (Bechtold and Patterson 2005). This report summarizes vegetation community data collected at Timucuan Ecological and Historic Preserve and Fort Caroline National Memorial in 2009.

1. Data were collected at 26 spatially-balanced random locations at the Preserve. The findings below apply only to portions of the park that meet the following site selection criteria:

    a) Sites are located within park boundaries and ownership.

    b) Sites must be sampleable within safety guidelines.

    c) Sites cannot be located in wholly non-natural areas, open water, or areas where application of the methods is inappropriate (such as marshes).

2. Sampling activities occurred at the Preserve from 6/22–6/26/2009, 6/29–7/2/2009, 7/13–7/17/2009, and 7/23–7/29/2009.

3. Monitoring efforts resulted in the addition of 11 species, subspecies, or varieties to the park's species list.

4. Absolute canopy cover across the park was approximately 63%.

5. Live oak (*Quercus virginiana*) had the largest average diameter at breast height of any canopy species at the park.

6. Gallberry (*Ilex glabra*) was the most frequent seedling detected ($0.63/m^2$).

7. Of canopy-sized redbay (*Persea borbonia*) measured, 73% were standing dead. Live redbay occurred in the shrub stratum in approximately half of the sites sampled. Redbay seedlings were detected at a frequency of $0.08/m^2$.

8. Saw palmetto was the most frequently occurring species in the shrub stratum.

9. Gallberry, bracken fern (*Pteridium aquilinum*), poison ivy (*Toxicodendron radicans*), and muscadine (*Vitis rotundifolia*) were the most frequently occurring species in the groundcover stratum.

10. Saw palmetto (*Serenoa repens*) had the highest absolute cover in the shrub stratum, while gallberry (*Ilex glabra*) had the highest relative cover in the shrub stratum.

11. Bracken fern had the highest absolute and relative cover in the groundcover stratum.

12. The full dataset, and associated metadata, can be acquired from the data store at http://science.nature.nps.gov/nrdata/.

Introduction

Overview

Vegetation communities provide many ecosystem services. Among their many functions, they are an important component of food webs and wildlife habitat for many species, and serve as a carbon sink, produce oxygen, cycle nutrients and energy through an ecosystem, influence the local climate, improve water quality, and moderate flooding and erosion. Plant communities also respond to multiple stressors such as changes in air quality, hydrology, disturbance regimes, and climate. Determining trends in vegetation communities is vital to understanding the ecological processes occurring at a site, and identifying stressors and their impacts.

Vegetation communities are dynamic entities with constant changes in composition, cover, distribution, and structure that reflect stressor response, natural or anthropogenic in origin. Disturbance is the primary stressor and regulating mechanism of SECN vegetation communities. The timing, type, and extent of the disturbance generally evokes a distinguishable response in the species composition, diversity, and structure of the landscape (Foster et al. 1998, Turner et al. 1990). The primary natural-disturbance processes in SECN parks are fire and weather (e.g., hurricanes, drought). Anthropogenic influences include fire suppression, landscape fragmentation, altered hydrology, and non-native species introduction.

The SECN is composed of a diverse assemblage of vegetation communities. Approximately 180 vegetation associations (i.e., fine-resolution floristic description), as defined by the National Vegetation and Classification System (FGDC 2008), occur in the SECN. These communities vary widely in distribution, species composition, and structure, and include sparsely vegetated primary dune communities, late successional old-growth bottomland hardwood forest communities, and highly diverse herbaceous-dominated mesic pine savannah communities.

Given the widespread anthropogenic influences in SECN parks and the importance of vegetation communities, quantifying trends in plant cover, frequency, diversity, and distribution is a high priority (DeVivo et al. 2008). Evaluating trends in these metrics provides measures for assessing the ecological integrity and sustainability of southeastern ecosystems, and identifying the need for specific management activities on our park lands. The National Park Service Omnibus Management Act of 1998, and other reinforcing policies and regulations, require park managers "to establish baseline information and to provide information on the long-term trends in the condition of National Park System resources" (Title II, Sec. 204). The vegetation-community monitoring data summarized herein is a tool to assist park managers in fulfilling this mandate.

This report summarizes data collected as a part of the SECN's Vegetation Community Vital Signs monitoring efforts.

Monitoring Objective

- Determine trends in plant species frequency, percent cover, diversity, and distribution in the groundcover, shrub, and canopy strata.

Methods

Study Area

Timucuan Ecological and Historic Preserve (TIMU) and Fort Caroline National Memorial (FOCA) are co-administered parks on the northeast Florida coast (Figure 1). The 18,616 ha (46,000 ac) TIMU encompasses the mouth of the St. Johns River and the lower several miles of the Nassau River. The Preserve is a collection of landowners (private, The Nature Conservancy, City of Jacksonville, Florida State Parks, federal), with approximately 3,440 ha (8,500 ac) of the Preserve under federal ownership. FOCA, also within the TIMU boundary, is 56 ha (138 ac). The Preserve consists of large areas of salt marsh that vary in degrees of salinity, but are generally dominated by smooth cordgrass (*Spartina alterniflora*) and needlegrass rush (*Juncus roemerianus*), some freshwater streams, ponds, and wetlands, and adjacent uplands. The uplands are a mosaic of maritime hammock that contain species such as live oak (*Quercus virginiana*), cabbage palm (*Sabal palmetto*); xeric hammock and coastal scrubs that contain and live oak (*Quercus geminata*), saw palmetto (*Serenoa repens*), and rusty fetterbush (*Lyonia ferruginia*); slash pine (*Pinus elliottii*) stands; and restored longleaf pine (*Pinus palustris*) stands.

During the last decade, the lands adjacent to the Preserve and Memorial have exhibited some of the most rapid growth and development in Florida. Consequently, the Preserve has a prominent wildland-urban interface and is host to many external stressors, including altered ecosystem function (e.g., fire suppression, hydrology), invasive species, and the direct and indirect effects of contaminants accrued throughout the watershed of the St. Johns River, Florida's longest river. Many of the upland

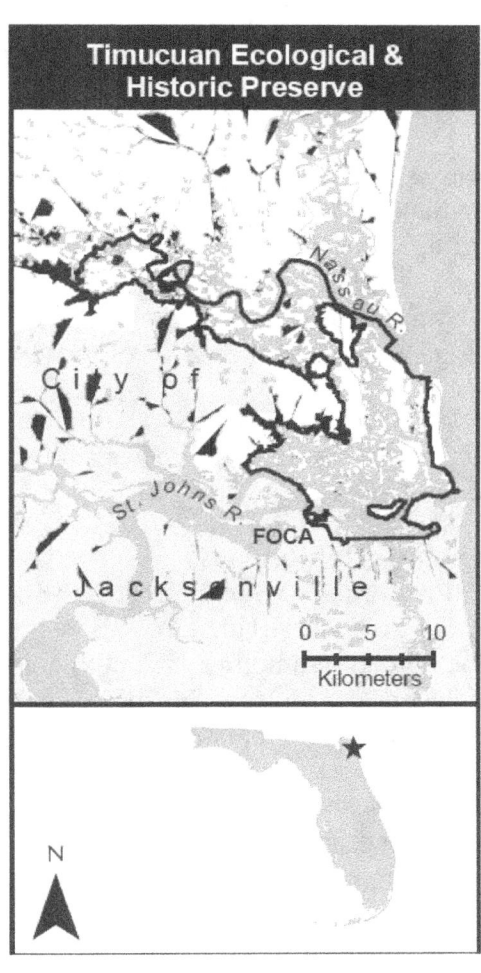

Figure 1. Location of Timucuan Ecological and Historic Preserve and Fort Caroline National Memorial.

communities evolved with frequent fires. Longleaf pine communities at the Preserve typically had fire-return intervals of 2–5 years and increasing fire suppression over the last several decades has had a marked impact on some of the uplands at the Preserve by increasing woody- / shrub-species density, reducing understory diversity, and increasing the likelihood of high-intensity fires. Despite this, the Preserve remains quite diverse and plays a crucial role in providing habitat for many rare species, including West Indian manatee (*Trichechus manatus*), painted bunting (*Passerina ciris*), gopher tortoise (*Gopherus polyphemus*), loggerhead sea turtle (*Caretta caretta*), hooded pitcher plant (*Sarracenia minor*) and is the northernmost extent for some sub-tropical plant species such as wild coffee (*Psychotria nervosa*) and snowberry (*Chiococca alba*).

The Preserve is threatened by several non-native invasive species, including tamarisk (*Tamarix* spp.), air potato (*Dioscorea bulbifera*), and privet (*Ligustrum* spp.).

Redbay are a critical native element of the coastal maritime hammock community and also serve as an important habitat component for many vertebrates, invertebrates, vascular plants, and non-vascular plants. Occurrences of native redbay (*Persea borbonia*) in the Preserve are in rapid decline due to the introduction of a fungal pathogen, laurel wilt (*Raffaelea lauricola*), whose vector is the non-native redbay ambrosia beetle (from Asia) (*Xyleborus glabratus*). Since the beetle's initial detection in 2002 (Haack 2006, Rabaglia 2003), and the subsequent lethality of laurel wilt to redbay, this pathogen has had a profound adverse effect on redbay across the Preserve and in over 60 counties in the southeastern U.S. (Fraedrich et al. 2008), primarily along the Atlantic coast (http://www.fs.fed.us/r8/foresthealth/laurelwilt/dist_map.shtml). Extensive multi-agency efforts are currently underway to further understand this pathogen, identify possible methods of eradication, and identify mitigation procedures to ensure the persistence of redbay and other potentially susceptible members of the Lauraceae. The breadth of the adverse ecological impacts of the loss of redbay in the coastal maritime hammock is unknown.

TIMU/FOCA has 624 known vascular-plant species, subspecies, and varieties (NPSpecies 2011), including 11 species, subspecies, and varieties added to the species based on these monitoring efforts (Appendix A, Table 2).

Sampling Design

To allow for park-wide inference, the park's administrative boundary was used as the sampling frame, which was divided into a systematic 0.5-ha grid; the center point of each grid cell served as the potential sampling site and the grid cell served as the macroplot. A spatially-balanced sample was drawn from this grid using the Reversed Randomized Quadrant-Recursive Raster (RRQRR) algorithm (Theobald et al. 2007). Alternate points were used when selection criteria (i.e., including safety and access issues) were not met. A sample size of 26 was chosen after consideration of park size, hypothesized variability, and logistical issues regarding travel time and conducting monitoring activities in five to six park units per year. The Preserve was sampled from 6/22–6/26, 6/29–7/2, 7/13–7/17, and 7/23–7/29/2009.

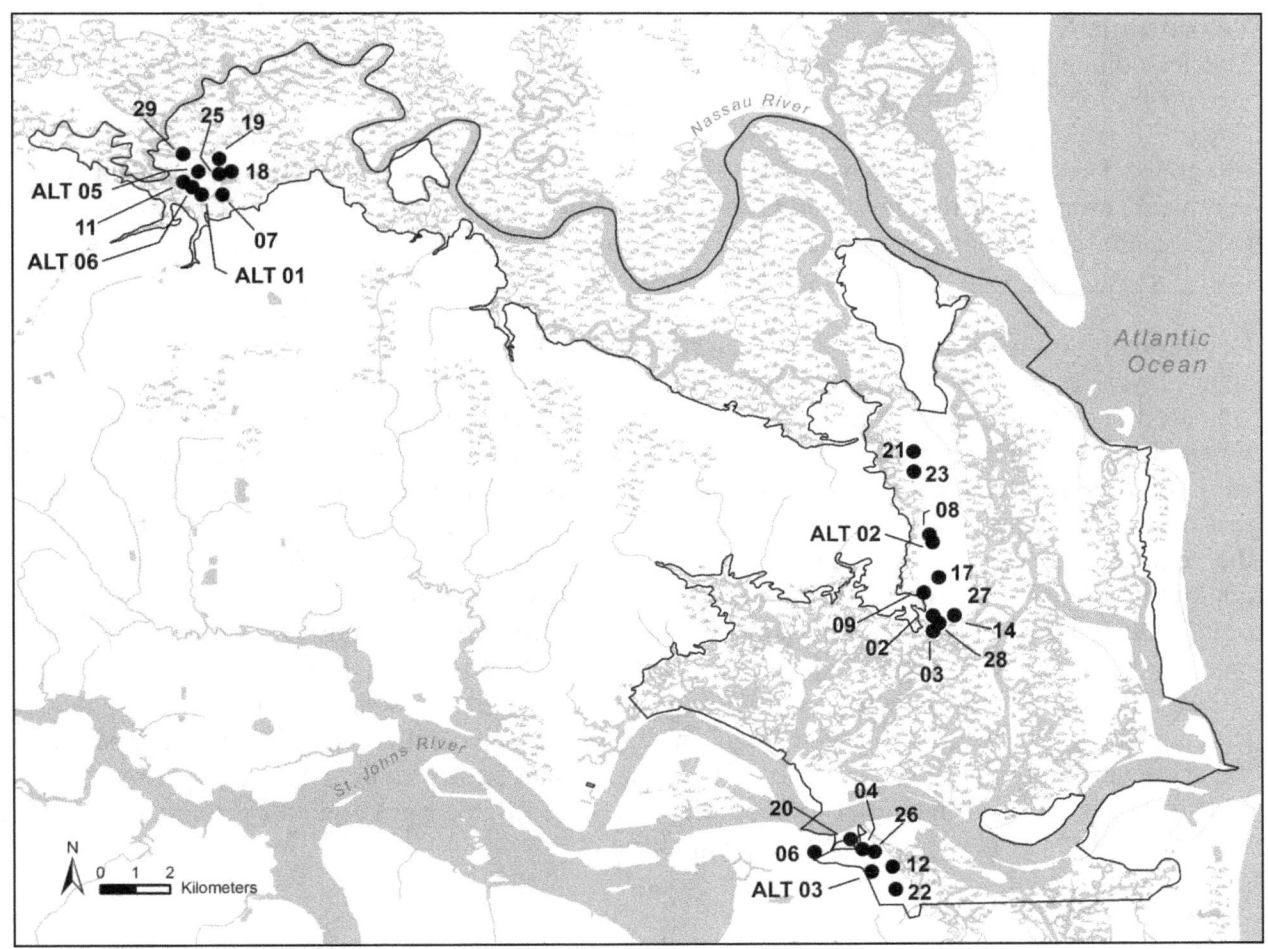

Figure 2. Spatially-balanced random sampling locations at Timucuan Ecological and Historic Preserve and Fort Caroline National Memorial, 2009.

Taxonomic Standards

Species nomenclature for this report follow the current NPSpecies database accessible through the Integration of Resource Management Applications (IRMA) portal (https://irma.nps.gov/App/Portal/Home), which represents the most recent updates from the Integrated Taxonomic Information System (ITIS; http://www.itis.gov). Standards used for the botanical taxonomy in this report and for all work conducted by the Southeast Coast Network (SECN) are in accordance with those set forth in by ITIS (http://irma.nps.gov/content/help/taxonomy/FAQ.aspx).

Occasionally, if the available characteristics of a plant did not facilitate identification to genus, species, variety, or subspecies, the lowest level of taxonomy identifiable (i.e., the most refined) was used. For example, species of *Dicanthelium* are extremely difficult to identify to species when they lack floral or fruiting structures. In this case, the specimen may only be identified to genus as *Dicanthelium* sp. In the event that a species has more than one variety or subspecies that occurs for a park and the specific variety or subspecies cannot be identified in the field, only the genus and species name were used. For example, several varieties of *Pteridium aquilinum* are known. If for some reason the observer was only able to identify the plant as *Pteridium aquilinum* and not further to variety, only *Pteridium aquilinum* was reported. In these cases, the identified and reported name may not be included in the existing park species list from NPSpecies, only the sub-species or varieties are included in the park species list. Because the genus or species is already known to occur in the park, the general taxonomy will not appear in the "new vascular plant species" (Table 2). In the event a family name, generic name, or genera and species name only (no variety, subspecies, etc.) is used, the most recent taxonomy represented in ITIS is used for these general terms.

Sampling Methodology

Vegetation community measures were divided into three strata based upon diameter at breast height (DBH) of woody species: canopy, shrub, and groundcover. Any non-woody (i.e., herbaceous) species was considered part of the groundcover stratum. Within each stratum, vegetation communities were sampled using a hybrid of methods used by the North Carolina Vegetation Survey nested-subplot design (Peet et al. 1998) within a circular plot similar to the Forest Inventory and Analysis protocol (Bechtold and Patterson 2005).

Plot Layout

The layout consisted of a circular plot with a radius of 15 m within the 0.5-ha macroplot. Subplots were systematically placed along six transects that radiated out from the center point at azimuths of 0°/360°, 60°, 120°, 180°, 240°, and 300° (Figure 3). To avoid overlap, subplots originated four meters from the macroplot (i.e., 0.5-ha grid) center point and extended away from the center point. Five measures were collected in the nested subplots within each plot: canopy cover, shrub cover, DBH, canopy-species seedling frequency, and herbaceous cover. Canopy cover was measured from the center point of the 0.5-ha macroplot. Shrub coverage was measured in two 2 × 4 m shrub plots along each transect. The shrub plots were further subdivided into 2 × 2 m subplots to improve cover-estimation accuracy and precision because cover-estimation error increases with plot size (solid gray shading, Figure 3). Groundcover coverage, groundcover nested frequency, and seedling frequency was measured in two 1 × 1 m groundcover plots (solid black shading, Figure 3) along each transect. Canopy species DBH was measured in three sections, each representing 1/3 of the total circular plot (hashed gray shading, Figure 3).

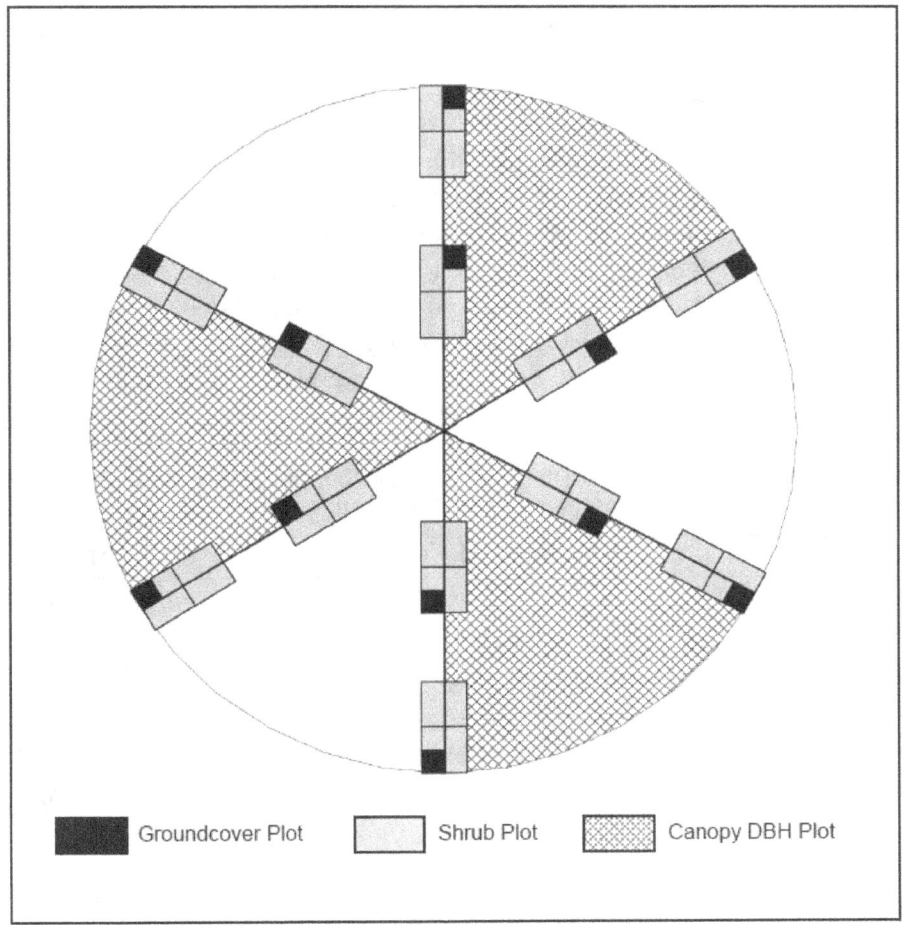

■ Groundcover Plot	☐ Shrub Plot	▨ Canopy DBH Plot

Figure 3. Southeast Coast Network vegetation-community monitoring plot layout.

Canopy Measures

Absolute canopy cover was estimated in the four cardinal directions with a concave spherical densiometer placed on a 1.1-m tall tripod at the plot center. Canopy cover reported is the mean of three observers across the four cardinal directions. The circular plot was subdivided into six sections occurring between the 0–60°, 120–180°, and 240–300° compass transects of the circular plot. Diameter at breast height (i.e., 1.37 m above the ground) was measured to the nearest millimeter for all trees (identified by species) with a diameter greater than or equal to 4 cm that occur within the 0–60°, 120–180°, and 240–300° section.

Shrub Measures

Shrub cover of all shrub species was visually estimated for each of the twelve 2 × 4 m plots. A common source of error in visual estimation of vegetation cover is that as plot size increases, cover-estimation error increases. Each shrub plot was therefore sub-divided into two 2 × 2 m subplots. The plots are situated at 15 m and 8 m (extending toward the plot center) along each of the transect lines of the circular plot. Shrub cover was categorized into one of seven coverage classes (Table 1) for each subplot. A coverage class of zero (Table 1) is assumed for any shrub species not detected and not recorded on the datasheet. The measurements of subplots were combined by averaging the midpoint for the coverage class in the two shrub subplots resulting in a total shrub cover estimate for the 2 × 4 m plot. The authors have established consistent performance in the accuracy and precision of visual-cover estimates within and across observers in plots this size.

Groundcover Measures

Groundcover was visually estimated in each of the twelve 1 × 1 m plots situated on the clockwise side at 15 m and 8 m (extending toward the plot center) along each of the transect lines of the circular plot. Groundcover was categorized into one of seven coverage classes (Table 1) for each plot. A coverage class of zero (Table 1) is assumed for any groundcover species not detected and not recorded on the datasheet. The authors have established through trials that these coverage classes are discriminatory and repeatable across observers. Canopy-species seedling counts were estimated by counting the number of seedlings that occur in each of the 1 × 1 m plots.

Table 1. Cover estimation coverage class, percent cover range, and value used for analyses for Southeast Coast Network vegetation-community monitoring protocol.

Coverage Class	Percent Cover Range	Value Used for Analyses
0	0%	0.0
1	Trace (<1%)	0.5
2	1-5%	2.5
3	5-25%	15.0
4	25-50%	37.5
5	50-75%	62.5
6	75-95%	85.0
7	95-100%	97.5

Data Analysis

Because this is the first year of this protocol's implementation at the Preserve, only the status of the elements presented in the aforementioned monitoring objective are determined, with the exception of diversity and distribution. The data in this report are presented by plot and pooled across plots. Sampling locations are presented in Figure 2 and summaries by plot are presented in Tables 3–9.

Summaries include (a) new species detected (Table 2),(b) canopy cover (Table 3), (c) canopy species size (Table 4), (d) seedling frequency (Table 5), (e) shrub species relative cover and frequency (Table 6), shrub species absolute cover and frequency (Table 7), (f) groundcover relative cover and frequency (Table 8), (g) groundcover absolute cover and frequency (Table 9), and (h) species detected (Appendix A).

Findings

We detected 137 species, subspecies, and varieties during this monitoring effort (Appendix A), including 11 new species, subspecies, and varieties not previously known to occur at TIMU/FOCA (Table 2).

Table 2. New vascular plant species detected at Timucuan Ecological and Historic Preserve and Fort Caroline National Memorial during 2009 monitoring efforts and recommended NPSpecies classifications.

Species	Abundance	Nativity	Pest	Management Priority	Exploitation Concerns
Asimina triloba	Unknown	Native	No	No	No
Cynodon dactylon	Unknown	Not Native	No	No	No
Itea virginica	Unknown	Native	No	No	No
Lemna minor	Unknown	Native	No	No	No
Morella caroliniensis	Unknown	Native	No	No	No
Nymphoides aquatica	Unknown	Native	No	No	No
Proserpinaca palustris	Unknown	Native	No	No	No
Quercus hemisphaerica	Unknown	Native	No	No	No
Sabatia grandiflora	Unknown	Native	No	No	No
Sideroxylon lycioides	Unknown	Native	No	No	No
Taxodium ascendens	Unknown	Native	No	No	No

Measures of Community Structure

Absolute canopy cover was variable across the all sampling locations at the park ($\bar{x}$ = 62.93%, SD = 33.17; Table 3). Live oak (*Quercus virginiana*) had the largest average DBH ($\bar{x}$ = 37.27 cm, SD = 36.25) of any species where more than ten individuals were sampled (Table 4). Average live redbay (*Persea borbonia*) DBH was 6.61 cm (SD = 2.07) and average standing dead redbay DBH was 6.63 cm (SD=2.29) (Table 4). Fifty-nine redbay individuals were measured, and of those 43 were standing dead (73%). Redbay seedlings were estimated at 0.08/m^2 (Table 5). Saw palmetto (*Serenoa repens*) was the most frequently occurring shrub species at the park (f = 61.54) and had the second highest relative cover of all shrub species ($\bar{x}$ = 14.58%, SD = 20.05; Table 6). Gallberry (*Ilex glabra*) had the highest relative cover of all shrub species ($\bar{x}$ = 15.39%, SD = 26.07; Table 6). Saw palmetto had the highest absolute cover in the shrub stratum at the park ($\bar{x}$ = 12.65%, SD = 17.58; Table 7) followed by gallberry ($\bar{x}$ = 11.86%, SD = 20.3; Table 7). Redbay occurred in the shrub stratum in almost half of the sampling locations and had an average realtive cover of 3.12% (SD = 6.18; Table 6). Gallberry (*Ilex glabra*) was the most frequently occurring species (38.5%) in the groundcover stratum (Table 8). Bracken fern (*Pteridium aquilinum*), poison ivy (*Toxicodendron radicans*), and muscadine grape (*Vitis rotundifolia*) were the second most frequently occurring species (34.6%) in the groundcover stratum (Table 8). Bracken fern had the highest absolute cover in the groundcover stratum ($\bar{x}$ = 2.74%, SD = 5.72; Table 9). Bracken fern also had the highest relative cover in the groundcover stratum ($\bar{x}$, = 3.25%, SD = 6.81; Table 8) followed by redroot (*Lachnanthes caroliana*) ($\bar{x}$ = 2.79%, SD = 6.33; Table 8).

Table 3. Average canopy cover in vegetation monitoring sampling locations at Timucuan Ecological and Historic Preserve and Fort Caroline National Memorial, 2009.

Site	Average Canopy Cover	Standard Deviation
TIMU-2	77.33	4.5
TIMU-3	88.75	2.05
TIMU-4	90.42	1.66
TIMU-6	84	3.68
TIMU-7	83.83	2.5
TIMU-8	28.33	3.26
TIMU-9	67.83	3.55
TIMU-11	2.75	1.32
TIMU-12	86.5	2.88
TIMU-14	90.5	1.75
TIMU-17	15.58	4.5
TIMU-18	86.5	2.18
TIMU-19	8.75	0.66
TIMU-20	85.67	3.75
TIMU-21	83.67	3.02
TIMU-23	90.08	1.04
TIMU-25	88	0.66
TIMU-26	44.08	3.21
TIMU-28	90.92	2.24
TIMU-29	25.58	1.81
TIMU-A1	12.25	1.27
TIMU-A2	66.92	2.27
TIMU-A3	82.08	3.75
TIMU-A5	3.58	0.58
TIMU-A6		
TIMU-22	89.25	2.65
Park Average	**62.93**	**33.17**

Table 4. Average canopy species size, measured as diameter (cm) at breast height (DBH) for species sampled in vegetation monitoring sampling locations at Timucuan Ecological and Historic Preserve and Fort Caroline National Memorial, 2009. Numbers in parentheses indicate the number of individual trees measured within each plot.

Species	Avg	Std Dev	2	3	4	6	7	8	9	11	12	14	17	18	19	20	21	22	23	25	26	28	29	A1	A2	A3	A5	A6
Acer rubrum	12.51	5.36					11.67 (10)													19.90 (1)						12.57 (3)		
Baccharis halimifolia	5.10															5.10 (1)												
Carya glabra	23.43	25.6	13.80 (1)	23.27 (6)								80.20 (1)						31.90 (3)				9.10 (5)						
Celtis laevigata	6.22	1.32		6.40 (4)																			5.85 (2)						
Diospyros virginiana	6.00	2.4												4.30 (1)			7.70 (1)												
Forestiera segregata	5.80				5.80 (1)																							
Gordonia lasianthus	10.93	7.73					7.94 (11)		6.92 (15)											9.64 (35) 19.18 (13)					11.65 (43)				
Ilex ambigua	5.98	2.16			5.98 (4)																							
Ilex cassine	7.95	2.46					8.10 (8)							6.90 (5)					7.43 (3)				4.20 (1)			10.26 (4)		
Ilex decidua	4.38	0.13			4.45 (2) 4.30 (2)																							
Ilex opaca	17.80	14.54			23.75 (2)																							
Ilex vomitoria	5.00	1.03			8.50 (1)																					5.90 (1)		
Juniperus virginiana	15.48	8.78	7.97 (3)	20.17 (6)																							
Liquidambar styraciflua	21.08	9.59					20.97 (12)				9.90 (1)					23.87 (6)											
Lyonia ferruginea	6.27	2.35				7.95 (2)		4.20 (1)					4.20 (1)				4.10 (2)		4.95 (2)	6.90 (6) 7.67 (3)					8.40 (1)			
Lyonia lucida	4.55	0.07																	4.55 (2)									
Magnolia grandiflora	15.17	8.55				12.99 (7)													29.30 (2)						8.70 (2)			
Magnolia virginiana	16.4	14.28					26.50 (1)																		6.30 (1)			
Morus rubra	7.63	2.62			8.90 (1)								8.50 (3)															
Myrica cerifera	5.62	1.15					5.63 (8)		5.73 (7)					5.20 (2)					5.88 (6)			5.70 (2)						
Nyssa sylvatica var. biflora	15.96	8.78					19.04 (14)								11.00 (3)					11.42 (9) 16.56 (21)							4.00 (1)		
Nyssa sylvatica var. sylvatica	12.8											12.80 (1)																
Osmanthus americanus	6.9	1.84				8.20 (1)		5.60 (1)													5.70 (1)							
Persea borbonia	6.61	2.07			8.53 (3)	6.40 (2)			5.20 (13)	4.00 (1)				7.01 (7)	5.10 (1)								4.00 (1)					
Persea palustris	6.81	3.47					7.50 (1)		4.70 (2)	5.95 (2)										5.60 (1)								
Pinus elliotti	12.19	9.41						17.75 (4)		7.20 (1)			16.57 (3) 12.85 (16) 5.85 (8)								44.20 (1)				5.45 (13) 10.21 (21)		10.73 (3) 7.64 (18)	4.15 (2)	
Pinus palustris	6.17	1.79							4.92 (5)							7.92 (5)												4.90 (2)	
Pinus serotina	20.7	6.37							20.70 (8)											20.70 (2)								
Pinus taeda	13.56	10.61	27.10 (1)							8.57 (6)														17.68 (4)				
Prunus serotina	13.54	5.96										9.20 (1)						13.20 (2)				14.54 (5)					
Quercus chapmanii	5.55	0.78																5.55 (2)										
Quercus geminata	7.11	3.83						5.15 (4)						5.27 (6)				6.60 (16)				11.60 (6)						
Quercus hemisphaerica	16.33	15.04				16.33 (10)																						
Quercus laurifolia	8.77	5.09							5.00 (1)			7.18 (16)				22.33 (3)	5.05 (8)	9.97 (13)	6.15 (2)			6.20 (1)						
Quercus myrtifolia	5.91	2.01						5.10 (1)					4.43 (3)					5.58 (25)				8.13 (6)						
Quercus nigra	8.63	4.97							6.69 (21)											12.53 (6) 28.10 (1)								
Quercus virginiana	37.27	36.25	41.79 (7)	77.70 (2) 16.98 (17)	18.40 (2)							117.25 (2)				42.07 (3)		62.40 (2)				83.00 (1)						
Sabal palmetto	34.16	10.33	42.96 (5)	25.37 (3)							29.13 (4) 26.20 (1)					45.60 (3)		22.40 (1)				28.15 (2)						
Taxodium ascendens	24.05	12.23																									24.05 (2)		
Vitis rotundifolia	5.43	1.26										5.83 (3)										4.20 (1)						
Vitis sp.	9.05	4.17										9.05 (2)																
Dead																												
Gordonia lasianthus	16.2						18.20 (1)																					
Ilex cassine	6.4					6.40 (1)																						
Juniperus virginiana	8.75	1.48													8.75 (2)													

Table 4. Continued.

Species	Avg	Std Dev	2	3	4	6	7	8	9	11	12	14	17	18	19	20	21	22	23	25	26	28	29	A1	A2	A3	A5	A6
Dead																												
Liquidambar styraciflua	7.3						7.30 (1)																					
Persea borbonia	6.63	2.29								4.78 (6)				7.18 (12)									7.18 (16)	5.86 (7)			
Persea palustris	10.61	4.71					12.39 (5)			6.25 (2)																		
Quercus sp	6.5													6.50 (1)														
unknown	12.24	7.44					12.24 (11)																					

Sampling Point

13

Table 5. Seedling frequency for canopy and shrub species in vegetation monitoring sampling locations at Timucuan Ecological and Historic Preserve and Fort Caroline National Memorial, 2009.

Species	Total Seedlings	Seedlings/m2	Std Dev	2	3	4	6	7	8	9	11	12	14	17	18	19	20	21	22	23	25	26	28	29	A1	A2	A3	A5	A6
Acer rubrum	9	0.03	0.06					0.08								0.33									0.17		0.17		
Amorpha fruticose	1	0	0.02	0.08																									
Andropogon virginicus var. glaucus	1	0	0.02																										
Baccharis halimifolia	3	0.01	0.04	0.08																0.08									
Borrichia frutescens	1	0	0.02	0.08																									
Callicarpa americana	2	0.01	0.03																				0.17						
Carya glabra	10	0.03	0.11		0.50								0.25						0.08										
Celtis laevigata	2	0.01	0.03		0.17																								
Cornus foemina	36	0.12	0.46										1.00										2.17						
Diospyros virginiana	1	0	0.02																					0.08					
Gaylussacia dumosa	12	0.04	0.14							0.17					0.50			0.50											
Gordonia lasianthus	5	0.02	0.04							0.17	0.08									0.08					0.08				
Hypericum sp.	5	0.02	0.07											0.08		0.33													
Ilex cassine	4	0.01	0.07					0.33																					
Ilex glabra	165	0.63	1.2							1.17	5.25			2.50	1.33								1.92	2.08	1.08		0.75	0.33	1.75
Ilex sp.	1	0	0.02			0.08																							
Ilex vomitoria	46	0.15	0.43	1.00	0.58								0.33										1.92						
Juniperus virginiana	2	0.01	0.03	0.17																									
Lyonia ferruginea	6	0.02	0.08								0.08										0.08								
Lyonia lucida	94	0.3	0.81					1.33						0.42						3.67	1.67								
Morella caroliniensis	1	0	0.02												0.08														
Morella cerifera	21	0.07	0.19			0.17		0.75							0.08	0.58		0.25											
Osmanthus americanus	1	0	0.02															0.08											
Persea borbonia	26	0.08	0.19		0.08	0.17	0.75								0.25							0.08	0.58	0.17		0.08		
Persea palustris	37	0.12	0.59					3.00											0.08								0.08		
Photinia pyrifolia	7	0.02	0.08								0.08				0.42										0.08				
Pinus elliottii	4	0.01	0.04												0.08							0.08		0.25	0.08				
Pinus taeda	3	0.01	0.05							0.25																			
Prunus caroliniana	6	0.02	0.1														0.50												
Prunus serotina	8	0.03	0.08		0.17								0.33										0.17					
Quercus geminata	11	0.04	0.13											0.50				0.42											
Quercus hemisphaerica	26	0.08	0.42	0.08	0.08		2.17																						
Quercus laurifolia	24	0.08	0.27			0.25							1.33	5.00				0.17	0.33										
Quercus myrtifolia	126	0.4	1.15			0.25								5.00				2.08				2.75							
Quercus nigra	3	0.01	0.05						0.42	0.25																			
Quercus virginiana	113	0.36	1.63	0.25	0.33	8.33	0.17					0.08	0.25																
Rhus copallina	2	0.01	0.02								0.08														0.08				
Sabal minor	2	0.01	0.03																	0.17									
Sabal palmetto	19	0.06	0.16	0.58	0.17								0.58								0.17		0.17					
Serenoa repens	1	0	0.02												0.08													
Symplocos tinctoria	1	0	0.02															0.08											
Vaccinium corymbosum	1	0	0.02																					0.08				
Vaccinium myrsinites	11	0.04	0.13											0.58				0.33											
Vitis rotundifolia	3	0.01	0.04										0.08					0.33					0.17						

Table 6. Percent of vegetation cover (relative cover) and frequency of occurrence of shrub species in vegetation monitoring sampling locations at Timucuan Ecological and Historic Preserve and Fort Caroline National Memorial, 2009.

Species	Frequency	Avg	Std Dev	2	3	4	6	7	8	9	11	12	14	17	18	19	20	21	22	23	25	26	28	29	A1	A2	A3	A5	A6
Acer rubrum	7.69	0.25	0.89																								3.13		
Amorpha fruticosa	3.85	0.23	1.16	5.91																									
Astrina sp	3.85	0.03	0.14								0.73																			
Astrina triloba	7.69	0.01	0.04		0.19								0.13																	
Baccharis angustifolia	3.85	0.06	0.29							1.50																				
Baccharis halimifolia	11.54	1.17	4.68									2.85		0.75		23.85														
Befaria racemosa	7.69	0.08	0.28						1.22	3.75																				
Borrichia frutescens	3.85	0.49	2.51	12.81																										
Callicarpa americana	11.54	0.06	0.19			0.64							0.16										0.77						
Carya glabra	11.54	0.35	1.31		1.16							1.47											6.52						
Celtis laevigata	3.85	0.04	0.23		1.16																								
Cephalanthus occidentalis	11.54	0.32	1.09					0.64							4.97		2.69												
Ceratiola ericoides	3.85	0.03	0.15																			0.76							
Cinnamomum camphora	3.85	0.03	0.14												0.69														
Cornus foemina	11.54	1.4	4.2										12.74						6.67				16.86						
Diospyros virginiana	15.38	1.25	3.81												3.93		17.51							6.66	2.43				
Erythrina herbacea	3.85	0.04	0.23		1.16																								
Euonymus americanus	3.85	0.05	0.28																1.43										
Gaylussacia dumosa	26.92	0.97	2.19					1.27		3.00				3.75				7.26		0.59		7.59				0.68		
Gordonia lasianthus	26.92	2.18	7.55							3.04					0.69					5.82	4.59							38.39		
Hamamelis virginiana	3.85	0.06	0.31				1.57																						
Ilex ambigua	7.69	0.27	1.05				5.12															1.79							
Ilex cassine	11.54	0.23	0.73					0.64													3.02						2.24		
Ilex decidua	3.85	0.15	0.75			3.82																							
Ilex glabra	46.15	15.39	26.07						1.22	37.08	65.85				21.36				1.78					50.28	53.38	8.00		66.03	81.24
Ilex sp	3.85	0.04	0.2											0.48															1.00
Ilex opaca	15.38	0.13	0.36			0.64			1.22				0.13																
Ilex vomitoria	30.77	2.65	5.85	25.12	2.31					1.50		12.78	2.73				7.07		5.24			12.28						
Itea virginica	3.85	1.93	9.83																							50.12		
Iva frutescens	3.85	0.17	0.87	4.43																								
Juniperus virginiana	11.54	0.41	1.51		2.31										0.92		7.41			2.47								
Leucothoe racemosa	3.85	0.09	0.48														9.09											
Liquidambar styraciflua	7.69	0.44	1.82					2.23						6.88				21.02										
Lyonia ferruginea	42.31	2.69	4.72				2.49		4.87	1.50										3.85	9.78	8.06			3.04	5.52		
Lyonia fruticosa	11.54	0.36	1.36				6.56		2.61					0.13														
Lyonia ligustrina	3.85	0.14	0.73							3.75																		
Lyonia lucida	26.92	4.48	11.73					48.74							0.69				27.02		28.38			5.07	3.49	3.13		
Magnolia grandiflora	7.69	0.13	0.46				1.57												1.79		0.72							
Magnolia virginiana	7.69	0.09	0.36												1.73													
Morus rubra	11.54	0.16	0.47		1.16								1.56									1.53						
Morella cerifera	50	7.41	14.07					44.36	1.04	8.11		35.38	4.46		14.78	48.26	20.54	3.09	0.71	9.37	0.72					1.94		
Nyssa sylvatica var. biflora	7.69	0.05	0.19												0.69						0.72							

15

Table 6. Continued.

Species	Frequency	Avg	Std Dev	Sampling Point																									
				2	3	4	6	7	8	9	11	12	14	17	18	19	20	21	22	23	25	26	28	29	A1	A2	A3	A5	A6
Osmanthus americanus	3.077	0.86	2.03			9.55	2.76		3.13					0.75	1.39			2.27				2.34							0.10
Persea borbonia	46.15	3.12	6.18		3.66	10.93	5.25			0.87	3.29	4.42			22.75		10.10		12.74	2.47		6.88	2.70	0.77	21.45	1.22			1.36	
Persea palustris	38.46	1.63	3.31					0.64		6.49					2.42	0.97												0.15		2.01
Photinia pyrifolia	7.69	0.19	0.69												2.08												2.03			
Pinus elliottii	23.08	2.4	5.26								10.13				2.77	17.47										18.05			8.36	
Pinus palustris	11.54	0.4	1.3								3.31					5.79													1.25	
Pinus taeda	3.85	0.28	1.42														2.36												
Prunus caroliniana	7.69	0.2	0.09																					7.24					
Prunus sp.	7.69	0.03	0.11			0.53																							
Ptelea trifoliata	3.85	0.05	0.26		1.35																								
Quercus chapmanii	3.85	0.02	0.08															0.41											
Quercus geminata	26.92	1.64	3.71						10.61					11.13				12.29							4.26			0.63	1.00
Quercus hemisphaerica	7.69	0.52	2.15				10.76											2.68											
Quercus laurifolia	11.54	0.99	4.48				1.97						0.91						22.86										
Quercus myrtifolia	19.23	4.89	12.29			2.87			13.74					39.38				28.91				42.36	0.14						
Quercus nigra	11.54	0.49	1.78							7.87					4.85														
Quercus virginiana	26.92	0.97	2.05	6.90		6.58	1.84					4.67					2.02		3.10										
Rhus copallina	26.92	0.83	1.81						0.17		2.19		0.13		0.69											5.49			4.81	2.04
Sabal minor	3.85	1.46	7.46																		38.04								
Sabal palmetto	34.62	13.21	26.12	44.83	84.39	1.27						38.33	81.51		3.12		5.05		23.81				61.25						
Sambucus canadensis	7.69	0.37	1.78			0.64											9.09												
Serenoa repens	61.54	14.58	20.05			39.81	39.63		58.96	23.85	10.74			21.50				13.60	11.79	43.59		16.91		3.13	0.20	71.25		10.97	0.19
Sideroxylon lycioides	3.85	0.03	0.15																			0.76							
Sideroxylon tenax	3.85	0.04	0.23		1.16																								
Sideroxylon sp.	3.85	0.16	0.78																4.05										
Symplocos tinctoria	3.85	0.13	0.66															3.37											
Tradica sebifera	3.85	0.03	0.14												0.69														
Vaccinium arboreum	11.54	1.32	4.33			7.01	20.47								4.62														
Vaccinium corymbosum	42.31	1.19	1.94					1.49		0.75	0.73									3.25	7.13				4.87	6.76	0.89	3.24	1.00
Vaccinium myrsinites	15.38	0.71	1.96											6.13				3.37				7.69							
Vaccinium sp.	3.85	0	0.02											0.13															
Vaccinium stamineum	11.54	0.6	1.96			8.07			1.22									1.30				6.22							
Unidentified																													
Magnoliopsida	7.69	0.13	0.56															0.41	2.86										

16

Table 7. Percent area covered (absolute cover) and frequency of occurrence of shrub species sampled in vegetation monitoring sampling locations at Timucuan Ecological and Historic Preserve and Fort Caroline National Memorial, 2009.

Species	Frequency	Avg	Std Dev	2	3	4	6	7	8	9	11	12	14	17	18	19	20	21	22	23	25	26	28	29	A1	A2	A3	A5	A6
Acer rubrum	7.69	0.11	0.45													0.73											2.19		
Amorpha fruticosa	3.85	0.1	0.49	2.50																									
Asimina sp.	3.85	0.02	0.12								0.63																		
Asimina triloba	7.69	0.01	0.03		0.10								0.10																
Baccharis angustifolia	3.85	0.05	0.25							1.25																			
Blechnum halophilum	11.54	0.36	1.16							3.13		1.25				5.10													
Befaria racemosa	7.69	0.05	0.18						0.73					0.63															
Borrichia frutescens	3.85	0.21	1.06	5.42																									
Callicarpa americana	11.54	0.05	0.17			0.63							0.13										0.63						
Carya glabra	11.54	0.25	1.05		0.63							0.63											5.31						
Celtis laevigata	3.85	0.02	0.12		0.63																								
Cephalanthus occidentalis	11.54	0.23	0.88					0.63							4.48		0.63												
Ceratiola ericoides	3.85	0.02	0.12																			0.63							
Cinnamomum camphora	3.85	0.02	0.12												0.63														
Cornus foemina	11.54	1.15	3.42										10.21		3.54		5.42		5.83				13.75						
Diospyros virginiana	15.38	0.64	1.71												3.54									6.95	1.25				
Erythrina herbacea	3.85	0.02	0.12		0.63																								
Euonymus americanus	3.85	0.05	0.25																1.25										
Gaylussacia dumosa	26.92	1.03	2.53					1.25						3.13	3.75			11.04		0.63		6.27				0.63		1.25	
Gordonia lasianthus	26.92	1.69	5.34				4.06			2.5	2.60				0.63					6.15	3.96	1.48					26.81		
Hamamelis virginiana	3.85	0.05	0.25				1.25																						
Ilex ambigua	7.69	0.21	0.84																		2.60	1.48							
Ilex cassine	11.54	0.18	0.59					0.63																			1.56		
Ilex decidua	3.85	0.14	0.74			3.75																							
Ilex glabra	46.15	11.86	20.3						0.73	30.94	56.35			7.92	19.27					1.88				36.88	28.44	7.4		67.81	50.63
Ilex sp.	3.85	0.02	0.12													0.10													0.63
Ilex opaca	15.38	0.1	0.3			0.63			0.73				0.10													1.25			
Ilex vomitoria	30.77	1.44	2.98	10.63	1.25					1.25		5.42	2.19				2.19		4.58				10.00						
Itea virginica	3.85	1.35	6.96																								35		
Iva frutescens	3.85	0.07	0.37	1.88																									
Juniperus virginiana	11.54	0.17	0.52		1.25										0.63		2.29												
Leucothoe racemosa	3.85	0.1	0.51																	2.60									
Liquidambar styraciflua	7.69	0.19	0.69					2.19									2.81												
Lyonia ferruginea	42.31	2.79	6.42			3.13	1.98			1.25				5.73				31.88		3.85	8.44	6.67			1.56	5.1			
Lyonia fruticosa	11.54	0.26	1.05				5.21		1.56					0.10															
Lyonia ligustrina	3.85	0.12	0.61							3.13																			
Lyonia lucida	26.92	4.21	11.42					47.83							0.63					28.54	24.48				2.6	3.23	2.19		
Magnolia grandiflora	7.69	0.11	0.38				1.25												1.98										
Magnolia virginiana	7.69	0.06	0.33												1.56						0.63								

17

Table 7. Continued.

Species	Frequency	Avg	Std Dev	2	3	4	6	7	8	9	11	12	14	17	18	19	20	21	22	23	25	26	28	29	A1	A2	A3	A5	A6
																									Sampling Point				
Morus rubra	11.54	0.12	0.35		0.63																								
Morella cerifera	50	4.52	9.17					43.54	0.63	0.77		15.00	1.25		13.33	10.42	6.35	4.69	0.63	9.90	0.63		1.25				1.35		
Nyssa sylvatica var biflora	7.69	0.05	0.17												0.63						0.63								
Osmanthus americanus	30.77	0.8	1.97			9.35	2.19		1.88					0.63	1.25			3.44				1.94						0.1	
Persea borbonia	46.15	2.59	5.22		1.98	10.73	4.17			0.73	2.81				20.52					2.23	5.94			15.73	0.63		0.1	1.35	
Persea palustris	38.46	1.1	2.44					0.63		5.42		1.88			2.19	0.21	3.13		11.15	2.60									1.25
Photinia pyrifolia	7.69	0.18	0.63												1.88											2.71			
Pinus elliotti	23.08	1.38	2.92								8.67				2.50	3.77									9.27			8.33	3.44
Pinus palustris	11.54	0.21	0.63								2.83					1.25												1.25	
Pinus taeda	3.85	0.2	1.04																					5.31					
Prunus caroliniana	7.69	0.12	0.49														0.73		2.40										
Prunus sp.	7.69	0.03	0.11			0.52													0.21										
Ptelea trifoliata	3.85	0.03	0.14		0.73																								
Quercus chapmanii	3.85	0.02	0.12															0.63											
Quercus geminata	26.92	1.54	4.12				8.54							9.27				18.65		2.33							0.63	0.63	
Quercus hemisphaerica	7.69	0.48	1.83				1.56						0.73					4.06											
Quercus laurifolia	11.54	0.86	3.92						8.23					32.81				43.85	20.00			35.02							
Quercus myrtifolia	19.23	4.72	12.2			2.81									4.38														
Quercus nigra	11.54	0.42	1.52							6.56							0.63							0.10					
Quercus virginiana	26.92	0.63	1.47						0.1		1.88	1.98			0.63				2.71					4.48	2.81			4.79	1.27
Rhus copallina	26.92	0.61	1.37	2.92		6.46	1.46						0.10																
Sabal minor	3.85	1.26	6.44										65.31																
Sabal palmetto	34.62	8.56	17.89	18.96	45.63	1.25						16.25					1.56		20.83		32.81		49.90	2.29	0.1				
Sambucus canadensis	7.69	0.13	0.56			0.63											2.81												
Serenoa repens	61.54	12.65	17.58			39.06	31.46		35.31	19.9	9.19			17.92	2.81		2.19	20.63	10.31	46.04		13.96			0.1	65.83		10.94	3.85
Sideroxylon lycioides	3.85	0.02	0.12																			0.63							
Sideroxylon tenax	3.85	0.02	0.12		0.63																								
Sideroxylon sp.	3.85	0.14	0.69																3.54										
Symplocos tinctoria	3.85	0.2	1															5.10											
Tradica tealifora	3.85	0.02	0.12												0.63														
Vaccinium arboreum	11.54	1.13	3.56			6.88	16.25	1.46																					
Vaccinium corymbosum	42.31	0.99	1.64								0.63				4.17					3.44	6.15			2.19	2.5	6.25	0.63	3.23	0.63
Vaccinium myrsinites	15.38	0.67	1.81						0.73					5.10				5.10				6.35							
Vaccinium sp.	3.85	0	0.02											0.10															
Vaccinium stamineum	11.54	0.58	1.84			7.92												1.98				5.15							
Unidentified																												
Magnoliopsida	7.69	0.12	0.5															0.63	2.50										

Table 8. Percent of vegetation cover (relative cover) and frequency of occurrence of groundcover species in vegetation monitoring sampling locations at Timucuan Ecological and Historic Preserve and Fort Caroline National Memorial, 2009.

Species	Frequency	Avg	Std Dev	Sampling Point																									
				2	3	4	6	7	8	9	11	12	14	17	18	19	20	21	22	23	25	26	28	29	A1	A2	A3	A5	A6
Acer rubrum	15.38	0.05	0.2					0.04																	0.09		0.13		
Amorpha fruticosa	3.85	0.01	0.06	0.30																									
Andropogon virginicus var. glaucus	30.77	2.09	4.09								4.13				4.68	12.68				0.39				2.67	7.45			14.26	8.14
Andropogon virginicus var. virginicus	11.54	0.4	1.19						3.83															4.51				2.14	
Aronopus sp.	3.85	0.02	0.12							0.34																			
Baccharis halimifolia	7.69	0.02	0.09	0.30																									
Befaria racemosa	3.85	0.02	0.12						0.62																				
Bidens sp.	3.85	0.02	0.12						0.62																				
Bignonia capreolata	15.38	0.54	1.86		6.04								0.25						7.58										
Borrichia frutescens	3.85	0.01	0.06	0.30																									
Callicarpa americana	3.85	0.1	0.49																				2.51					
Campsis radicans	3.85	0.89	4.55														23.19												
Carex sp.	7.69	0.01	0.03							0.17									0.05										
Carya glabra	11.54	0.11	0.36		1.53								1.07						0.23										
Celtis laevigata	7.69	0.02	0.06		0.21														0.23										
Centella asiatica	11.54	0.09	0.33								0.98														1.40			0.07	
Chasmanthium laxum	11.54	0.54	2.11	2.07	10.64							1.39																	
Cnidoscolus stimulosus	7.69	0.06	0.27		0.26							1.39																	
Cornus foemina	11.54	0.28	0.92										1.60						1.38				4.31						
Cynodon dactylon	3.85	0.83	4.24						21.60																				
Cyperus haspan	3.85	0	0.01													0.03													
Cyperus sp.	11.54	0.05	0.16	0.59					0.12					0.55															
Dichanthelium sp.	50	1.24	3.06	0.06			5.40		0.62	0.17	14.61	1.19		3.24	0.04									0.23	0.27				3.95
Desta teres	3.85	0.17	0.85						4.32																				
Diospyros virginiana	3.85	0	0.01																					0.03					
Elephantopus sp.	7.69	0.13	0.48		1.26																		2.15					
Erechtites hieracifolius	7.69	0.02	0.09													0.14									0.45				
Erigeron vernus	3.85	0.01	0.05						0.25																				
Euonymus americanus	3.85	0.02	0.09																0.46										
Eupatorium capillifolium	15.38	0.63	2.13			0.90			0.25							0.42									5.87				
Eupatorium sp.	11.54	0.09	0.31													0.64									1.35				
Eustachys petraea	3.85	0.07	0.35	1.78																									0.23
Fimbristylis caroliniana	3.85	0.08	0.41							2.07																			
Galactia elliottii	50	2.27	3.52			1.96			8.64	2.79	7.94			10.01	0.04	0.84		9.05				0.07		1.20	6.32			8.20	2.09
Galium sp.	7.69	0.01	0.05		0.04																								
Gaylussacia dumosa	15.38	0.23	0.69															1.19	0.28			3.10						0.36	
Gelsemium sempervirens	23.08	0.8	2.08								6.26				1.31										1.81			2.49	6.74
Gordonia lasianthus	19.23	0.27	0.87							1.03	0.32									0.19					1.35		4.23		

Table 8. Continued.

Species	Frequency	Avg	Std Dev	2	3	4	6	7	8	9	11	12	14	17	18	19	20	21	22	23	25	26	28	29	A1	A2	A3	A5	A6
Ilex glabra	38.46	1.15	2.6						0.62	1.07	12.45			4.03	3.59										1.17	1.13	2.21		0.43	3.25
Ilex sp.	3.85	0.01	0.03			0.15																							
Ilex vomitoria	26.92	0.77	2.09	3.62	2.60							0.20	0.36				0.27		3.26				9.69						
Ipomoea sp.	7.69	0.01	0.06	0.30																			0.07						
Itea virginica	3.85	0.24	1.21																									6.15		
Juncus sp.	7.69	0.03	0.12																						0.05				
Juniperus virginiana	3.85	0.01	0.07	0.36																									
Lachnanthea caroliniana	26.92	2.79	6.33								18.42				1.16	8.92									7.18	8.35			2.85	28.57
Lechnocaulon anceps	11.54	0.1	0.42													0.14										0.23			2.14	
Lemna minor	3.85	0.5	2.54					12.95																						
Lemna sp.	3.85	0	0.02														0.11												
Lonicera japonica	7.69	0.1	0.46													0.14													2.49	
Ludwigia sp.	3.85	0.01	0.03																					0.17					
Lyonia ferruginea	15.38	0.06	0.19			0.90								0.30							0.07	0.18							
Lyonia fruticosa	3.85	0.07	0.34				1.74																						
Lyonia lucida	23.08	0.7	2.03					0.84												7.77	7.09				0.23	2.04	0.32		
Melaleuca sp.	7.69	0.01	0.04		0.04								0.18																
Mikania scandens	7.69	0.06	0.32										0.04				1.64												
Mitchella repens	11.54	0.18	0.55			1.51	0.67												2.30										
Morella caroliniensis	3.85	0.01	0.04												0.19														
Morella cerifera	19.23	0.14	0.36			0.18		1.34				0.20				0.98		0.99											
Nymphoidea aquatica	3.85	0.02	0.08					0.42																					
Optismenus hirtellus	7.69	0.07	0.26		1.28													0.10						0.43					
Osmanthus americanus	3.85	0	0.02																										
Osmunda cinnamomea	30.77	1.26	2.28							2.59					6.74	5.02					7.37				2.00	1.81			5.35	
Osmunda regalis	3.85	0.07	0.36													1.81													
Panicum hemitomon	11.54	1.2	4.61													6.92				0.19						22.11			
Panicum sp.	11.54	0.02	0.06		0.04										0.19	0.28													
Parthenocissus quinquefolia	26.92	0.16	0.57									0.20	0.18				0.05		0.46				2.87				0.38		
Paspalum notatum	7.69	1.51	6.8						34.57						4.68														
Paspalum sp.	3.85	0.07	0.35	1.78																									
Passiflora incarnata	3.85	0.16	0.8														4.09												
Passiflora lutea	7.69	0.01	0.04	0.06	0.21																								
Persea borbonia	30.77	0.4	1.32		0.21	6.10									0.22							0.07	3.23	0.17		0.06			
Persea palustris	15.38	0.11	0.49			0.33		2.51																				0.36	
Photinia pyrifolia	15.38	0.04	0.11								0.32				0.37				0.23	0.04							0.06		
Phytolacca americana	3.85	0.16	0.8												0.04		4.09								0.05				
Pinus elliottii	11.54	0.03	0.14																					0.20				0.71	
Pinus taeda	3.85	0.01	0.04																										
Polygala lutea	7.69	0.03	0.09													0.42													0.23

Table 8. Continued.

Species	Frequency	Avg	Std Dev	2	3	4	6	7	8	9	11	12	14	17	18	19	20	21	22	23	25	26	28	29	A1	A2	A3	A5	A6
Polypremum procumbens	3.85	0.33	1.69						8.64																				
Proserpinaca palustris	3.85	0.01	0.05													0.28												
Prunus caroliniana	7.69	0.01	0.05														0.27		0.05										
Prunus serotina	11.54	0.02	0.07		0.21								0.25										0.14						
Pteridium aquilinum	34.62	3.25	6.81			1.81			0.62		22.55			1.00	1.12			0.99						16.37	6.09			18.53	16.50
Quercus geminata	11.54	0.2	0.84											2.99				0.99				1.12							
Quercus hemisphaerica	3.85	0.7	3.59				18.29																						
Quercus laurifolia	19.23	0.14	0.42	0.06	0.21								1.10					0.50	1.84										
Quercus myrtifolia	19.23	0.91	2.59			0.15			0.62					4.78				8.25				9.91							
Quercus nigra	3.85	0.01	0.07							0.34																			
Quercus virginiana	26.92	0.47	1.24		1.53	5.73		1.74				2.46	0.21				0.27												
Rhexia sp.	11.54	0.02	0.05								0.06					0.14								0.17					
Rhus copallina	7.69	0.02	0.07								0.32																		
Rhynchospora megalocarpa	3.85	0.2	1.02				5.23																					0.23	
Rhynchospora sp.	34.62	0.33	0.68						0.62		2.35			1.74	0.04	0.31								0.17	0.32				0.93
Richardia brasiliensis	3.85	0	0.02						0.12																				
Rivina humilis	3.85	0.01	0.06	0.30																									
Rubus sp.	23.08	0.52	1.69			0.15											7.64		4.36				1.08	0.20				0.07	
Ruellia caroliniensis	15.38	0.61	1.68	4.45	1.91														7.16				2.23					
Sabal minor	3.85	0.08	0.43																		2.18							
Sabal palmetto	26.92	0.7	1.72	3.62	1.49							0.04	2.31						3.03				7.54						
Sabatia grandiflora	3.85	0.01	0.08						0.32						0.19														
Sambucus canadensis	3.85	0.03	0.18			0.90																							
Scleria triglomerata	26.92	0.95	2.1				0.87				6.99								1.38					1.00	2.71				
Serenoa repens	15.38	0.12	0.4	1.81						1.03				0.10												0.06			
Smilax auriculata	7.69	0.07	0.24		0.64								1.07																
Smilax bona-nox	23.08	0.54	1.92		1.49							1.23						9.69							1.35				
Smilax glauca	30.77	0.43	1.21			5.12				3.62				0.35						1.35	0.07			0.20				0.43	0.05
Smilax laurifolia	15.38	0.1	0.36	1.78				0.04														0.04						
Smilax pumila	15.38	1	4.64			1.99	23.09																					
Smilax sp.	11.54	1.86	9.47														48.28												
Solidago sp.	11.54	0.26	0.91				10.34			3.86				0.05				0.30				0.07						
Sporobolus virginicus	3.85	0.17	0.87	4.45										2.99														
Symplocos tinctoria	3.85	0.02	0.1												0.19			0.50										
Toxicodendron radicans	34.62	1.61	4.62	0.59	1.28		15.68						8.21				20.89				0.35		9.76		0.23		0.32	0.36
Vaccinium arboreum	3.85	0.6	3.07											0.85				0.69							0.23				
Vaccinium corymbosum	3.85	0.01	0.04																			0.54							
Vaccinium myrsinites	15.38	0.1	0.24						0.62													0.22						0.54	
Vaccinium stamineum	3.85	0.01	0.04													0.14												0.22	
Viola lanceolata ssp. occidentalis	7.69	0.02	0.1													0.14									0.50				
Vitis aestivalis	3.85	0.33	1.66														8.46												
Vitis rotundifolia	34.62	1.64	4.2							0.38			0.04				1.64	5.05		2.90			9.69			1.75	1.92		
Wahlenbergia marginata	3.85	0.02	0.12						0.62																				
Woodwardia areolata	11.54	1.14	4.27												8.23	0.84											20.50		
Woodwardia virginica	3.85	0.12	0.59																					3.01				2.21	
Xyris sp.	11.54	0.1	0.43													0.28									0.05				

Table 8. Continued.

Species	Frequency	Avg	Std Dev	2	3	4	6	7	8	9	11	12	14	17	18	19	20	21	22	23	25	26	28	29	A1	A2	A3	A5	A6
Unidentified																													
Asteraceae	19.23	0.39	1.34		0.21				5.68				0.04			4.04									0.23				
Cucurbitaceae	3.85	0.06	0.42																				2.15						
Fabaceae	11.54	0.11	0.35	0.89	0.26														1.61										
Filicopsida	3.85	0.01	0.07																										
Magnoliopsida	15.38	0.28	1.18			5.68			0.12							1.17								0.33					
Lamiaceae	11.54	0.04	0.13								0.32					0.56								0.03					
Poaceae	15.38	0.31	1.02						4.94											0.19				0.20	1.35				
Tracheobionta	3.85	0.01	0.03				0.17							1.49															
Ground Condition																													
Aquatic or obligate non-vascular	19.23	0.23	0.59													2.09				0.19	0.35						1.92		1.39
Bare Ground	23.08	1.25	3.34	1.78												10.45						0.18						12.12	
Exposed Humus	11.54	0.31	1.33					1.25				0.20		7.72								0.04					6.73		
Leaf Litter or Duff	84.62	47.05	30.17	67.87	66.38	70.52		34.04		80.72		76.86	63.13	56.27	43.79	25.91		77.53	26.86	76.73	63.55	84.32	42.07	53.11	17.60	89.45	53.49	16.04	16.97
Open Water	34.62	5.06	9.81					41.77				14.66			21.89				8.89	18.96			5.68	8.80				9.07
Tree Stump	3.85	0.17	0.86																								4.37			
Upland non-vascular plants or lichens	15.38	0.29	0.95					4.59						1.49					1.16		0.18								

22

Table 9. Percent area covered (absolute cover) and frequency of occurrence by groundcover species sampled in vegetation monitoring sampling locations at Timucuan Ecological and Historic Preserve and Fort Caroline National Memorial, 2009.

Species	Frequency	Avg	Std Dev	2	3	4	6	7	8	9	11	12	14	17	18	19	20	21	22	23	25	26	28	29	A1	A2	A3	A5	A6
Acer rubrum	15.38	0.07	0.29					0.04																	0.08		0.08		
Aenophia fruticosa	3.85	0.01	0.04	0.25																									
Andropogon virginicus var. glaucus	30.77	2.04	4.32								2.71				5.21	18.96				0.42				3.33	6.88			8.33	7.29
Juniperus virginicus var. virginicus	11.54	0.31	1.14						1.29																			1.25	
Atropogus sp.	3.85	0.01	0.04						0.21																				
Baccharis halimifolia	7.69	0.02	0.09	0.21						0.42																			
Befaria racemosa	3.85	0.01	0.04						0.21																				
Bidens sp.	3.85	0.01	0.04						0.21																				
Bignonia capreolata	15.38	0.5	1.74		5.92								0.29																
Borrichia frutescens	3.85	0.01	0.04	0.21															6.88										
Callicarpa americana	3.85	0.06	0.29																				1.46						
Campsis radicans	3.85	0.68	3.47														17.71												
Carex sp.	7.69	0.01	0.04							0.21									0.04										
Carya glabra	11.54	0.11	0.38		1.50								1.25						0.21										
Celtis laevigata	7.69	0.02	0.06		0.21														0.21										
Centella asiatica	11.54	0.11	0.37													1.46									1.29			0.04	
Chasmanthium laxum	11.54	0.51	2.06	1.46	10.42							1.46																	
Chidioscolus stimulosus	7.69	0.07	0.29		0.25							1.46																	
Cornus foemina	11.54	0.22	0.64						7.29				1.88						1.25										
Cynodon dactylon	3.85	0.28	1.43																				2.50						
Cyperus haspan	3.85	0	0.01													0.04													
Cyperus sp.	11.54	0.04	0.12	0.42					0.04					0.46															
Dichanthelium sp.	50	0.82	2	0.04			1.29		0.21	0.21	9.58	1.25		2.71					1.46					0.29	0.25			0.50	3.54
Diodia teres	3.85	0.06	0.29						1.46																				
Diospyros virginiana	3.85	0	0.01												0.04									0.04					
Elephantopus sp.	7.69	0.1	0.34		1.25																		1.25						
Erechtites hieracifolius	7.69	0.02	0.09													0.21									0.42				
Erigeron vernus	3.85	0	0.02						0.08																				
Euonymus americanus	3.85	0.02	0.08																0.42										
Eupatorium capillifolium	15.38	0.8	2.92						0.08							14.08									5.42				
Eupatorium sp.	11.54	0.1	0.34			1.25										1.25									1.25			1.25	
Eustachys petraea	3.85	0.05	0.25	1.25																									
Fimbristylis caroliniana	3.85	0.1	0.49							2.50																			
Galactia elliottii	50	1.61	2.33			2.71			2.92	3.38	5.21			8.36	0.04	1.25		3.79				0.08		1.50	5.83			4.79	1.88
Galium sp.	7.69	0.01	0.05		0.04														0.25										
Gaylussacia dumosa	15.38	0.22	0.75												1.46			0.50				3.58						0.21	
Gelsemium sempervirens	23.08	0.63	1.58								5.42				1.46	0.21									1.67				6.04
Gordonia lasianthus	19.23	0.22	0.62																	0.21							2.75		
Hamamelis virginiana	3.85	0.01	0.04				0.21																						
Hypericum cistifolium	3.85	0	0.01						0.04																				
Hypericum sp.	15.38	0.09	0.34											0.04		1.71									0.21				0.42

23

Table 9. Continued.

Species	Frequency	Avg	Std Dev	2	3	4	6	7	8	9	11	12	14	17	18	19	20	21	22	23	25	26	28	29	A1	A2	A3	A5	A6
Ilex ambigua	3.85	0	0.01																										
Ilex cassine	3.85	0.01	0.04					0.21														0.04							
Ilex glabra	38.46	0.93	1.87					0.21	0.21	1.29	8.17			3.38										1.46	1.04	1.58		0.25	2.92
Ilex sp.	3.85	0.01	0.04			0.21																							
Ilex vomitoria	26.92	0.56	1.35	2.54								0.21	0.42				0.21		2.96				5.63						
Ipomoea sp.	7.69	0.01	0.04	0.21																			0.04						
Itea virginica	3.85	0.15	0.76																								4.00		
Juncus sp.	7.69	0.01	0.04						0.21																0.04				
Juniperus virginiana	3.85	0.01	0.05	0.25																									
Lachnanthes caroliana	26.92	2.61	5.71								12.08				1.29	13.33								8.96	7.71			1.87	22.92
Lachnocaulon anceps	11.54	0.06	0.25													0.21									0.21			1.25	
Lemna minor	3.85	0.5	2.53					12.92																					
Lemna sp.	3.85	0	0.02														0.08												
Lonicera japonica	7.69	0.06	0.29													0.21												1.46	
Ludwigia sp.	3.85	0.01	0.04																					0.21					
Lyonia ferruginea	15.38	0.07	0.25											0.25							0.04								
Lyonia fruticosa	3.85	0.02	0.08				0.42															0.21							
Lyonia lucida	23.08	0.59	1.81					0.83												8.38	4.21					1.46	0.21		
Maianea sp.	7.69	0.01	0.04		0.04								0.21																
Mikania scandens	7.69	0.05	0.24										0.04				1.25												
Michelia repens	11.54	0.17	0.57			2.08	0.21												2.08										
Morella caroliniensis	3.85	0.01	0.04												0.21														
Morella cerifera	19.23	0.14	0.36		0.25			1.33				0.21				1.46		0.42											
Nymphoides aquatica	3.85	0.02	0.08					0.42																					
Oplismenus hirtellus	7.69	0.06	0.25		1.25																		0.25						
Osmanthus americanus	3.85	0	0.01															0.04											
Osmunda cinnamomea	30.77	1.19	2.23							3.13					7.50	7.50					4.35			2.50	1.87		1.25	3.13	
Osmunda regalis	3.85	0.1	0.53													2.71													
Panicum hemitomon	11.54	1.31	4.69													13.33				0.21									
Panicum sp.	11.54	0.03	0.09												0.21				0.04										
Parthenocissus quinquefolia	26.92	0.11	0.33		0.04							0.21	0.21		0.21	0.42	0.04		0.42				1.67				0.25		
Paspalum notatum	7.69	0.65	2.47						11.67						5.21														
Paspalum sp.	3.85	0.05	0.25	1.25													3.13												
Passiflora incarnata	3.85	0.12	0.61														3.13												
Passiflora lutea	3.85	0	0.01	0.04																									
Passiflora lutea	3.85	0.01	0.04		0.21																								
Persea borbonia	30.77	0.18	0.46		0.21	0.46									0.25							0.08	1.88	0.21		0.04	0.04		
Persea palustris	15.38	0.11	0.49				1.46	2.50											0.21	0.04									
Photinia pyrifolia	15.38	0.03	0.1								0.21				0.42													0.21	
Phytolacca americana	3.85	0.12	0.61														3.13												
Pinus elliotii	11.54	0.02	0.06												0.04										0.04			0.42	
Pinus taeda	3.85	0.01	0.05																					0.25					
Polygala lutea	7.69	0.03	0.13													0.63													0.21
Polypremum procumbens	3.85	0.11	0.57						2.92																				
Proserpinaca palustris	3.85	0.02	0.08													0.42													
Prunus caroliniana	7.69	0.01	0.04														0.21		0.04										

Table 9. Continued.

Species	Frequency	Avg	Std Dev	2	3	4	6	7	8	9	11	12	14	17	18	19	20	21	22	23	25	26	28	29	A1	A2	A3	A5	A6
Prunus serotina	11.54	0.02	0.07		0.21								0.29										0.08						
Pteridium aquilinum	34.62	2.74	5.72			2.50			0.21		14.79			0.83	1.25									20.42	5.63			10.83	14.79
Quercus geminata	11.54	0.16	0.54											2.50				0.42				1.29							
Quercus hemisphaerica	3.85	0.17	0.86				4.38																						
Quercus laurifolia	19.23	0.13	0.4	0.04	0.21								1.29					0.21	1.67										
Quercus myrtifolia	19.23	0.74	2.41			0.21			0.21					4.00				3.46				11.46							
Quercus nigra	3.85	0.02	0.08							0.42																			
Quercus virginiana	26.92	0.5	1.62	0.21	1.50	7.92	0.42					2.58	0.25			0.21													
Rhexia sp.	11.54	0.02	0.06								0.04																		
Rhus copallina	7.69	0.02	0.08								0.21					0.21								0.21					
Rhynchospora megalocarpa	3.85	0.05	0.25					1.25																					
Rhynchospora sp.	34.62	0.25	0.48	1.46					0.21		1.54			1.46	0.04	0.46								0.21	0.29				0.83
Richardia brasiliensis	3.85	0	0.01						0.04																				
Rivina humilis	3.85	0.01	0.04	0.21																									
Rubus sp.	23.08	0.42	1.35			0.21											5.63		3.96				0.63	0.25		0.04		
Ruellia caroliniensis	15.38	0.49	1.43	3.13	1.88														6.50				1.29					
Sabal minor	3.85	0.05	0.25																		1.29							
Sabal palmetto	26.92	0.54	1.18	2.54	1.46							0.04	2.71		0.21				2.75				4.38					
Sambucus grandiflora	3.85	0.01	0.04								0.21																		
Sambucus canadensis	3.85	0.05	0.26			1.25																						
Scleria triglomerata	26.92	0.69	1.43			0.21					4.58			0.08					1.25					1.25	2.50			4.38	3.75
Serenoa repens	15.38	0.15	0.54			2.50				1.25																0.04			
Smilax auriculata	7.69	0.07	0.27		0.63								1.25																
Smilax bona-nox	23.08	0.5	1.75	0.21	1.46							1.29							8.79						1.25			0.04	
Smilax glauca	30.77	0.53	1.6			7.08				4.38				0.29						1.46	0.04			0.25				0.25	
Smilax lauriifolia	15.38	0.07	0.25	1.25				0.04			0.42														0.04				0.04
Smilax pumila	15.38	0.33	1.21			2.75	5.67											0.13				0.04						
Smilax sp.	11.54	1.42	7.23											0.04			36.86						0.04					
Solidago sp.	11.54	0.27	0.98							4.42				2.50	0.21														
Sporobolus virginicus	3.85	0.12	0.61	3.13																									
Symplocos tinctoria	3.85	0.01	0.04																										
Toxicodendron radicans	34.62	1.41	4.17	0.42	1.25								9.63					0.21	18.96		0.21		5.67		0.21		0.21		
Vaccinium arboreum	3.85	0.14	0.74				3.75																						
Vaccinium corymbosum	3.85	0.01	0.04																						0.21				
Vaccinium myrsinites	15.38	0.07	0.19						0.21					0.71				0.25				0.63							
Vaccinium stamineum	3.85	0.01	0.05																			0.25							
Viola lanceolata ssp. occidentalis	7.69	0.03	0.1													0.21									0.46				
Vitis aestivalis	3.85	0.25	1.27														6.46												
Vitis rotundifolia	34.62	0.65	1.67				4.63			0.46			0.04				1.25		4.58	3.13			5.63			1.25	1.25		
Wahlenbergia marginata	3.85	0.01	0.04						0.21																				
Woodwardia areolata	11.54	0.91	3.11												9.17	1.25											13.33		
Woodwardia virginica	3.85	0.14	0.74																					3.75					
Xyris sp.	11.54	0.07	0.26													0.42									0.04				1.29

Table 9. Continued.

				Sampling Point																									
Species	Frequency	Avg	Std Dev	2	3	4	6	7	8	9	11	12	14	17	18	19	20	21	22	23	25	26	28	29	A1	A2	A3	A5	A6
Woodwardia areolata	11.54	0.91	3.11												9.17	1.25											13.33		
Woodwardia virginica	3.85	0.14	0.74																					3.75					
Xyris sp	11.54	0.07	0.26													0.42									0.04			1.29	
Unidentified																												
Asteraceae	19.23	0.32	1.23		0.21				1.92				0.04			6.04									0.21				
Cucurbitaceae	3.85	0.05	0.25																				1.25						
Fabaceae	11.54	0.09	0.31	0.63	0.25														1.48										
Filicopsida	3.85	0.02	0.08																					0.42					
Magnoliopsida	15.38	0.38	1.62			8.13			0.04							1.75													
Lamiaceae	11.54	0.05	0.17								0.21					0.83								0.04					
Poaceae	15.38	0.17	0.46						1.67					1.25						0.21					1.25				
Tracheobionta	3.85	0	0.01				0.04																						
Ground Condition																												
Aquatic or obligate non-vascular plants	19.23	0.23	0.68													3.13				0.21	0.21								1.25
Bare Ground	23.08	1.19	3.47	1.25												15.63						0.21						7.08	
Exposed Humus	11.54	0.22	0.88					1.25				0.21		6.46								0.04					4.38		
Leaf Litter or Duff	84.62	44.6	33.09	47.71	65.00	97.50		33.96		97.50		60.83	97.50	47.06	48.75	38.75		32.50	24.38	82.71	37.71	97.50	24.42	66.25	16.25	63.96	34.79	9.38	15.21
Open Water	34.62	4.68	9.7					41.67				15.42			24.38					9.58	11.25			7.08	8.13				8.13
Tree Stump	3.85	0.12	0.61																							3.13			
Upland Non-Vascular plants or Lichens	15.38	0.28	0.94					4.58						1.25						1.25		0.21							

26

Literature Cited

Bechtold, W. A. and P. L. Patterson, (eds.). 2005. The enhanced forest inventory and analysis program — national sampling design and estimation procedures. General Technical Report SRS-80. USDA Forest Service, Southern Research Station, Asheville, NC. 85 pp.

Byrne, M. W. 2009. Sampling-point generation for SECN monitoring protocols: Generating a spatially-balanced random sample with the RRQRR tool in ArcGIS 9.1. Draft Standard Operating Procedure Version 1.0, last updated March 2009.

DeVivo, J. C., C. J. Wright, M. W. Byrne, E. DiDonato, and T. Curtis. 2008. Vital signs monitoring in the Southeast Coast Inventory & Monitoring Network. Natural Resource Report NPS/SECN/NRR—2008/061. USDI National Park Service, Fort Collins, CO, USA.

Fraedrich S. W., T. C. Harrington, R. J. Rabaglia, M. D. Ulyshen, A. E. Mayfield III, J. L. Hanula, J. M. Eickwort, and D. R. Miller. 2008. A fungal symbiont of the redbay ambrosia beetle causes a lethal wilt in redbay and other Lauraceae in the southeastern United States. Plant Disease 92:215–224.

Federal Geographic Data Committee. 2008. National vegetation classification standard, version 2. FGDC-STD-005-2008. Available online: http://www.fgdc.gov/standards/project/FGDC-standards-projects/vegetation.

Foster, D. R., G. Motzkin, and B. Slater. 1998. Land-use history as long-term broad-scale disturbance: regional forest dynamics in central New England. Ecosystems: 1:96-119.

Haack, R. A. 2006. Exotic bark- and wood-boring Coleoptera in the United States: Recent establishments and interceptions. Canadian Journal of Forest Research 36:269-288.

NPSpecies - The National Park Service Biodiversity Database. Secure online version. https://science1.nature.nps.gov/npspecies/web/main/start (Park list: accessed 1/13/2011).

Peet R. K., T. R. Wentworth, and P. S White. 1998. A flexible, multipurpose method for recording vegetation composition and structure. Castanea 63:262-274.

Rabaglia, R. 2003. *Xyleborus glabratus*. Online record, URL: http://spfnic.fs.fed.us/exfor/data/pestreports.cfm?pestidval=148&langdisplay=english (Accessed 2/14/2012).

Theobald, D. M., D. L. Stevens, D. White, N. S. Urquhart, A. R. Olsen, and J. B. Norman. 2007. Using GIS to generate spatially balanced random survey designs for natural resource applications Environmental Management 40:134-146.

Turner, II, B. L., W. C. Clark, R. W. Kates, J. F. Richards, J. T. Mathews, and W. B. Meyer, (eds.). 1990. The earth as transformed by human action: Global and regional changes in the biosphere over the past 300 years. Cambridge University Press, Cambridge, UK.

Appendix A. Plant species known to occur at Timucuan Ecological and Historic Preserve and Fort Caroline National Memorial.

Table A-1. Vascular plant species known occur at Timucuan Ecological and Historic Preserve and Fort Caroline National Memorial (NPSpecies 2011) and species detected during 2009 monitoring efforts.

Order	Family	Species	NPSpecies	This Study
Scrophulariales	Acanthaceae	*Justicia brandegeeana*	X	
Scrophulariales	Acanthaceae	*Odontonema cuspidatum*	X	
Scrophulariales	Acanthaceae	*Ruellia caroliniensis*	X	X
Scrophulariales	Acanthaceae	*Stenandrium dulce*	X	
Sapindales	Aceraceae	*Acer rubrum*	X	X
Liliales	Agavaceae	*Yucca aloifolia*	X	
Liliales	Agavaceae	*Yucca filamentosa*	X	
Caryophyllales	Aizoaceae	*Sesuvium portulacastrum*	X	
Caryophyllales	Aizoaceae	*Tetragonia tetragonioides*	X	
Alismatales	Alismataceae	*Sagittaria filiformis*	X	
Alismatales	Alismataceae	*Sagittaria graminea var. graminea*	X	
Caryophyllales	Amaranthaceae	*Alternanthera philoxeroides*	X	
Caryophyllales	Amaranthaceae	*Iresine rhizomatosa*	X	
Sapindales	Anacardiaceae	*Rhus copallina*	X	X
Sapindales	Anacardiaceae	*Rhus copallinum*	X	
Sapindales	Anacardiaceae	*Toxicodendron radicans*	X	X
Magnoliales	Annonaceae	*Asimina angustifolia*	X	
Magnoliales	Annonaceae	*Asimina incana*	X	
Magnoliales	Annonaceae	*Asimina parviflora*	X	
Magnoliales	Annonaceae	*Asimina pygmea*	X	
Magnoliales	Annonaceae	*Asimina triloba*		X
Apiales	Apiaceae	*Centella asiatica*	X	X
Apiales	Apiaceae	*Cicuta maculata*	X	
Apiales	Apiaceae	*Cyclospermum leptophyllum*	X	
Apiales	Apiaceae	*Eryngium aromaticum*	X	
Apiales	Apiaceae	*Eryngium baldwinii*	X	
Apiales	Apiaceae	*Hydrocotyle bonariensis*	X	
Apiales	Apiaceae	*Hydrocotyle umbellata*	X	
Apiales	Apiaceae	*Sanicula canadensis*	X	
Apiales	Apiaceae	*Spermolepis divaricata*	X	
Celastrales	Aquifoliaceae	*Ilex ambigua*	X	X
Celastrales	Aquifoliaceae	*Ilex ambigua var. ambigua*	X	
Celastrales	Aquifoliaceae	*Ilex cassine*	X	X
Celastrales	Aquifoliaceae	*Ilex cassine var. cassine*	X	
Celastrales	Aquifoliaceae	*Ilex cassine var. myrtifolia*	X	
Celastrales	Aquifoliaceae	*Ilex decidua*	X	X
Celastrales	Aquifoliaceae	*Ilex glabra*	X	X
Celastrales	Aquifoliaceae	*Ilex opaca*	X	X
Celastrales	Aquifoliaceae	*Ilex opaca var. opaca*	X	
Celastrales	Aquifoliaceae	*Ilex vomitoria*	X	X
Arales	Araceae	*Arisaema dracontium*	X	
Apiales	Araliaceae	*Aralia spinosa*	X	
Apiales	Araliaceae	*Hedera helix*	X	

Table A-1. Continued

Order	Family	Species	NPSpecies	This Study
Arecales	Arecaceae	*Sabal minor*	X	X
Arecales	Arecaceae	*Sabal palmetto*	X	X
Arecales	Arecaceae	*Serenoa repens*	X	X
Aristolochiales	Aristolochiaceae	*Aristolochia serpentaria*	X	
Gentianales	Asclepiadaceae	*Asclepias cinerea*	X	
Gentianales	Asclepiadaceae	*Asclepias curassavica*	X	
Gentianales	Asclepiadaceae	*Asclepias humistrata*	X	
Gentianales	Asclepiadaceae	*Asclepias tomentosa*	X	
Gentianales	Asclepiadaceae	*Asclepias tuberosa*	X	
Gentianales	Asclepiadaceae	*Cynanchum angustifolium*	X	
Gentianales	Asclepiadaceae	*Cynanchum scoparium*	X	
Polypodiales	Aspleniaceae	*Asplenium platyneuron*	X	
Polypodiales	Aspleniaceae	*Asplenium resiliens*	X	
Asterales	Asteraceae	*Ambrosia artemisiifolia*	X	
Asterales	Asteraceae	*Baccharis angustifolia*	X	X
Asterales	Asteraceae	*Baccharis halimifolia*	X	X
Asterales	Asteraceae	*Balduina angustifolia*	X	
Asterales	Asteraceae	*Balduina uniflora*	X	
Asterales	Asteraceae	*Berlandiera pumila*	X	
Asterales	Asteraceae	*Bidens alba*	X	
Asterales	Asteraceae	*Bidens bipinnata*	X	
Asterales	Asteraceae	*Bidens mitis*	X	
Asterales	Asteraceae	*Bigelowia nudata ssp. nudata*	X	
Asterales	Asteraceae	*Borrichia frutescens*	X	X
Asterales	Asteraceae	*Carphephorus corymbosus*	X	
Asterales	Asteraceae	*Carphephorus odoratissimus*	X	
Asterales	Asteraceae	*Chrysopsis mariana*	X	
Asterales	Asteraceae	*Cirsium horridulum*	X	
Asterales	Asteraceae	*Cirsium nuttallii*	X	
Asterales	Asteraceae	*Conoclinium coelestinum*	X	
Asterales	Asteraceae	*Conyza canadensis*	X	
Asterales	Asteraceae	*Conyza canadensis var. pusilla*	X	
Asterales	Asteraceae	*Coreopsis basalis*	X	
Asterales	Asteraceae	*Cyanthillium cinereum*	X	
Asterales	Asteraceae	*Eclipta prostrata*	X	
Asterales	Asteraceae	*Elephantopus elatus*	X	
Asterales	Asteraceae	*Elephantopus nudatus*	X	
Asterales	Asteraceae	*Erechtites hieraciifolius*	X	X
Asterales	Asteraceae	*Erigeron quercifolius*	X	
Asterales	Asteraceae	*Erigeron vernus*	X	X
Asterales	Asteraceae	*Eupatorium album*	X	
Asterales	Asteraceae	*Eupatorium capillifolium*	X	X
Asterales	Asteraceae	*Eupatorium leptophyllum*	X	
Asterales	Asteraceae	*Eupatorium mohrii*	X	
Asterales	Asteraceae	*Eupatorium rotundifolium*	X	
Asterales	Asteraceae	*Eupatorium serotinum*	X	
Asterales	Asteraceae	*Euthamia caroliniana*	X	
Asterales	Asteraceae	*Euthamia minor*	X	
Asterales	Asteraceae	*Gaillardia pulchella*	X	
Asterales	Asteraceae	*Gamochaeta falcata*	X	
Asterales	Asteraceae	*Gamochaeta pensylvanica*	X	

Table A-1. Continued

Order	Family	Species	NPSpecies	This Study
Asterales	Asteraceae	*Helenium pinnatifidum*	X	
Asterales	Asteraceae	*Helianthus angustifolius*	X	
Asterales	Asteraceae	*Heterotheca subaxillaris*	X	
Asterales	Asteraceae	*Hypochaeris brasiliensis var. tweedii*	X	
Asterales	Asteraceae	*Iva frutescens*	X	X
Asterales	Asteraceae	*Iva imbricata*	X	
Asterales	Asteraceae	*Iva microcephala*	X	
Asterales	Asteraceae	*Krigia virginica*	X	
Asterales	Asteraceae	*Lactuca floridana*	X	
Asterales	Asteraceae	*Liatris graminifolia*	X	
Asterales	Asteraceae	*Liatris spicata*	X	
Asterales	Asteraceae	*Liatris tenuifolia var. quadriflora*	X	
Asterales	Asteraceae	*Liatris tenuifolia var. tenuifolia*	X	
Asterales	Asteraceae	*Lygodesmia aphylla*	X	
Asterales	Asteraceae	*Melanthera nivea*	X	
Asterales	Asteraceae	*Mikania cordifolia*	X	
Asterales	Asteraceae	*Mikania scandens*	X	X
Asterales	Asteraceae	*Palafoxia integrifolia*	X	
Asterales	Asteraceae	*Pityopsis graminifolia*	X	
Asterales	Asteraceae	*Pluchea foetida*	X	
Asterales	Asteraceae	*Pluchea rosea*	X	
Asterales	Asteraceae	*Pterocaulon virgatum*	X	
Asterales	Asteraceae	*Pyrrhopappus carolinianus*	X	
Asterales	Asteraceae	*Sericocarpus tortifolius*	X	
Asterales	Asteraceae	*Smallanthus uvedalia*	X	
Asterales	Asteraceae	*Smallanthus uvedalius*	X	
Asterales	Asteraceae	*Solidago fistulosa*	X	
Asterales	Asteraceae	*Solidago odora var. chapmanii*	X	
Asterales	Asteraceae	*Solidago sempervirens*	X	
Asterales	Asteraceae	*Sonchus asper*	X	
Asterales	Asteraceae	*Sonchus oleraceus*	X	
Asterales	Asteraceae	*Symphyotrichum tenuifolium*	X	
Asterales	Asteraceae	*Taraxacum officinale*	X	
Asterales	Asteraceae	*Verbesina virginica*	X	
Asterales	Asteraceae	*Vernonia gigantea*	X	
Asterales	Asteraceae	*Youngia japonica*	X	
Batales	Bataceae	*Batis maritima*	X	
Fagales	Betulaceae	*Carpinus caroliniana*	X	
Scrophulariales	Bignoniaceae	*Bignonia capreolata*	X	X
Scrophulariales	Bignoniaceae	*Campsis radicans*	X	X
Scrophulariales	Bignoniaceae	*Macfadyena unguis-cati*	X	
Polypodiales	Blechnaceae	*Woodwardia areolata*	X	X
Polypodiales	Blechnaceae	*Woodwardia virginica*	X	X
Capparales	Brassicaceae	*Cardamine hirsuta*	X	
Capparales	Brassicaceae	*Descurainia pinnata*	X	
Capparales	Brassicaceae	*Lepidium virginicum*	X	
Bromeliales	Bromeliaceae	*Tillandsia bartramii*	X	
Bromeliales	Bromeliaceae	*Tillandsia recurvata*	X	
Bromeliales	Bromeliaceae	*Tillandsia usneoides*	X	
Scrophulariales	Buddlejaceae	*Polypremum procumbens*	X	X
Caryophyllales	Cactaceae	*Opuntia pusilla*	X	

Table A-1. Continued

Order	Family	Species	NPSpecies	This Study
Caryophyllales	Cactaceae	*Opuntia stricta*	X	
Campanulales	Campanulaceae	*Lobelia glandulosa*	X	
Campanulales	Campanulaceae	*Triodanis perfoliata*	X	
Campanulales	Campanulaceae	*Wahlenbergia marginata*	X	X
Dipsacales	Caprifoliaceae	*Lonicera japonica*	X	X
Dipsacales	Caprifoliaceae	*Lonicera sempervirens*	X	
Dipsacales	Caprifoliaceae	*Sambucus canadensis*	X	X
Dipsacales	Caprifoliaceae	*Sambucus nigra ssp. canadensis*	X	
Dipsacales	Caprifoliaceae	*Viburnum odoratissimum*	X	
Caryophyllales	Caryophyllaceae	*Cerastium glomeratum*	X	
Caryophyllales	Caryophyllaceae	*Silene antirrhina*	X	
Caryophyllales	Caryophyllaceae	*Spergularia salina*	X	
Caryophyllales	Caryophyllaceae	*Stellaria media*	X	
Caryophyllales	Caryophyllaceae	*Stipulicida setacea*	X	
Celastrales	Celastraceae	*Euonymus americanus*	X	X
Caryophyllales	Chenopodiaceae	*Atriplex cristata*	X	
Caryophyllales	Chenopodiaceae	*Chenopodium album*	X	
Caryophyllales	Chenopodiaceae	*Chenopodium ambrosioides*	X	
Caryophyllales	Chenopodiaceae	*Salicornia virginica*	X	
Caryophyllales	Chenopodiaceae	*Sarcocornia perennis*	X	
Caryophyllales	Chenopodiaceae	*Suaeda linearis*	X	
Rosales	Chrysobalanaceae	*Licania michauxii*	X	
Violales	Cistaceae	*Helianthemum corymbosum*	X	
Violales	Cistaceae	*Lechea torreyi*	X	
Theales	Clusiaceae	*Hypericum brachyphyllum*	X	
Theales	Clusiaceae	*Hypericum cistifolium*	X	X
Theales	Clusiaceae	*Hypericum fasciculatum*	X	
Theales	Clusiaceae	*Hypericum gentianoides*	X	
Theales	Clusiaceae	*Hypericum hypericoides*	X	
Theales	Clusiaceae	*Hypericum mutilum*	X	
Theales	Clusiaceae	*Hypericum myrtifolium*	X	
Theales	Clusiaceae	*Hypericum reductum*	X	
Theales	Clusiaceae	*Hypericum tetrapetalum*	X	
Theales	Clusiaceae	*Triadenum virginicum*	X	
Commelinales	Commelinaceae	*Callisia graminea*	X	
Commelinales	Commelinaceae	*Callisia ornata*	X	
Commelinales	Commelinaceae	*Commelina caroliniana*	X	
Commelinales	Commelinaceae	*Commelina erecta*	X	
Commelinales	Commelinaceae	*Gibasis pellucida*	X	
Commelinales	Commelinaceae	*Tradescantia ohiensis*	X	
Solanales	Convolvulaceae	*Dichondra carolinensis*	X	
Solanales	Convolvulaceae	*Ipomoea alba*	X	
Solanales	Convolvulaceae	*Ipomoea cordatotriloba*	X	
Solanales	Convolvulaceae	*Ipomoea pandurata*	X	
Solanales	Convolvulaceae	*Ipomoea sagittata*	X	
Solanales	Convolvulaceae	*Stylisma patens*	X	
Cornales	Cornaceae	*Cornus asperifolia*	X	
Cornales	Cornaceae	*Cornus foemina*	X	X
Violales	Cucurbitaceae	*Melothria pendula*	X	
Pinales	Cupressaceae	*Juniperus silicicola*	X	
Pinales	Cupressaceae	*Juniperus virginiana*	X	X

Table A-1. Continued

Order	Family	Species	NPSpecies	This Study
Cycadales	Cycadaceae	*Cycas revoluta*	X	
Cyperales	Cyperaceae	*Carex albicans*	X	
Cyperales	Cyperaceae	*Carex atlantica ssp. capillacea*	X	
Cyperales	Cyperaceae	*Carex glaucescens*	X	
Cyperales	Cyperaceae	*Carex striata*	X	
Cyperales	Cyperaceae	*Carex vulpinoidea*	X	
Cyperales	Cyperaceae	*Cladium jamaicense*	X	
Cyperales	Cyperaceae	*Cyperus croceus*	X	
Cyperales	Cyperaceae	*Cyperus erythrorhizos*	X	
Cyperales	Cyperaceae	*Cyperus esculentus*	X	
Cyperales	Cyperaceae	*Cyperus esculentus*	X	
Cyperales	Cyperaceae	*Cyperus haspan*	X	X
Cyperales	Cyperaceae	*Cyperus odoratus*	X	
Cyperales	Cyperaceae	*Cyperus polystachyos*	X	
Cyperales	Cyperaceae	*Cyperus retrorsus*	X	
Cyperales	Cyperaceae	*Eleocharis acicularis*	X	
Cyperales	Cyperaceae	*Eleocharis baldwinii*	X	
Cyperales	Cyperaceae	*Eleocharis flavescens*	X	
Cyperales	Cyperaceae	*Eleocharis vivipara*	X	
Cyperales	Cyperaceae	*Fimbristylis autumnalis*	X	
Cyperales	Cyperaceae	*Fimbristylis caroliniana*	X	X
Cyperales	Cyperaceae	*Fuirena breviseta*	X	
Cyperales	Cyperaceae	*Fuirena scirpoidea*	X	
Cyperales	Cyperaceae	*Rhynchospora caduca*	X	
Cyperales	Cyperaceae	*Rhynchospora colorata*	X	
Cyperales	Cyperaceae	*Rhynchospora fascicularis*	X	
Cyperales	Cyperaceae	*Rhynchospora inundata*	X	
Cyperales	Cyperaceae	*Rhynchospora megalocarpa*	X	X
Cyperales	Cyperaceae	*Rhynchospora microcephala*	X	
Cyperales	Cyperaceae	*Rhynchospora plumosa*	X	
Cyperales	Cyperaceae	*Scleria ciliata var. ciliata*	X	
Cyperales	Cyperaceae	*Scleria oligantha*	X	
Cyperales	Cyperaceae	*Scleria reticularis*	X	
Cyperales	Cyperaceae	*Scleria triglomerata*	X	X
Polypodiales	Dennstaedtiaceae	*Pteridium aquilinum*	X	X
Polypodiales	Dennstaedtiaceae	*Pteridium aquilinum var. pseudocaudatum*	X	
Liliales	Dioscoreaceae	*Dioscorea bulbifera*	X	
Nepenthales	Droseraceae	*Drosera capillaris*	X	
Nepenthales	Droseraceae	*Drosera intermedia*	X	
Polypodiales	Dryopteridaceae	*Nephrolepis exaltata*	X	
Ebenales	Ebenaceae	*Diospyros virginiana*	X	X
Ericales	Empetraceae	*Ceratiola ericoides*	X	X
Ericales	Ericaceae	*Befaria racemosa*	X	X
Ericales	Ericaceae	*Gaylussacia dumosa*	X	X
Ericales	Ericaceae	*Gaylussacia nana*	X	
Ericales	Ericaceae	*Gaylussacia tomentosa*	X	
Ericales	Ericaceae	*Kalmia hirsuta*	X	
Ericales	Ericaceae	*Leucothoe racemosa*	X	X
Ericales	Ericaceae	*Lyonia ferruginea*	X	X
Ericales	Ericaceae	*Lyonia fruticosa*	X	X
Ericales	Ericaceae	*Lyonia ligustrina*	X	X

Table A-1. Continued

Order	Family	Species	NPSpecies	This Study
Ericales	Ericaceae	*Lyonia ligustrina var. foliosiflora*	X	
Ericales	Ericaceae	*Lyonia lucida*	X	X
Ericales	Ericaceae	*Rhododendron canescens*	X	
Ericales	Ericaceae	*Vaccinium arboreum*	X	X
Ericales	Ericaceae	*Vaccinium corymbosum*	X	X
Ericales	Ericaceae	*Vaccinium darrowii*	X	
Ericales	Ericaceae	*Vaccinium myrsinites*	X	X
Ericales	Ericaceae	*Vaccinium stamineum*	X	X
Eriocaulales	Eriocaulaceae	*Eriocaulon decangulare*	X	
Eriocaulales	Eriocaulaceae	*Lachnocaulon anceps*	X	X
Eriocaulales	Eriocaulaceae	*Syngonanthus flavidulus*	X	
Euphorbiales	Euphorbiaceae	*Acalypha gracilens*	X	
Euphorbiales	Euphorbiaceae	*Chamaesyce hirta*	X	
Euphorbiales	Euphorbiaceae	*Chamaesyce hyssopifolia*	X	
Euphorbiales	Euphorbiaceae	*Chamaesyce maculata*	X	
Euphorbiales	Euphorbiaceae	*Cnidoscolus stimulosus*	X	X
Euphorbiales	Euphorbiaceae	*Croton glandulosus*	X	
Euphorbiales	Euphorbiaceae	*Croton glandulosus var. glandulosus*	X	
Euphorbiales	Euphorbiaceae	*Euphorbia heterophylla*	X	
Euphorbiales	Euphorbiaceae	*Phyllanthus abnormis*	X	
Euphorbiales	Euphorbiaceae	*Phyllanthus tenellus*	X	
Euphorbiales	Euphorbiaceae	*Phyllanthus urinaria*	X	
Euphorbiales	Euphorbiaceae	*Poinsettia cyathophora*	X	
Euphorbiales	Euphorbiaceae	*Stillingia sylvatica*	X	
Euphorbiales	Euphorbiaceae	*Tragia urens*	X	
Euphorbiales	Euphorbiaceae	*Triadica sebifera*	X	X
Fabales	Fabaceae	*Aeschynomene viscidula*	X	
Fabales	Fabaceae	*Albizia julibrissin*	X	
Fabales	Fabaceae	*Amorpha fruticosa*	X	X
Fabales	Fabaceae	*Amphicarpaea bracteata*	X	
Fabales	Fabaceae	*Centrosema virginianum*	X	
Fabales	Fabaceae	*Cercis canadensis*	X	
Fabales	Fabaceae	*Chamaecrista fasciculata*	X	
Fabales	Fabaceae	*Chamaecrista nictitans var. aspera*	X	
Fabales	Fabaceae	*Chamaecrista nictitans var. nictitans*	X	
Fabales	Fabaceae	*Clitoria mariana*	X	
Fabales	Fabaceae	*Crotalaria rotundifolia*	X	
Fabales	Fabaceae	*Desmodium glabellum*	X	
Fabales	Fabaceae	*Desmodium incanum*	X	
Fabales	Fabaceae	*Desmodium paniculatum*	X	
Fabales	Fabaceae	*Erythrina herbacea*	X	X
Fabales	Fabaceae	*Galactia elliottii*	X	X
Fabales	Fabaceae	*Galactia regularis*	X	
Fabales	Fabaceae	*Galactia volubilis*	X	
Fabales	Fabaceae	*Glottidium vesicarium*	X	
Fabales	Fabaceae	*Indigofera hirsuta*	X	
Fabales	Fabaceae	*Indigofera tinctoria*	X	
Fabales	Fabaceae	*Lupinus diffusus*	X	
Fabales	Fabaceae	*Medicago lupulina*	X	
Fabales	Fabaceae	*Melilotus alba*	X	
Fabales	Fabaceae	*Melilotus indicus*	X	

Table A-1. Continued

Order	Family	Species	NPSpecies	This Study
Fabales	Fabaceae	*Pueraria montana*	X	
Fabales	Fabaceae	*Strophostyles helvola*	X	
Fabales	Fabaceae	*Trifolium repens*	X	
Fabales	Fabaceae	*Vicia acutifolia*	X	
Fabales	Fabaceae	*Wisteria sinensis*	X	
Fagales	Fagaceae	*Castanea pumila*	X	
Fagales	Fagaceae	*Quercus chapmanii*	X	X
Fagales	Fagaceae	*Quercus elliottii*	X	
Fagales	Fagaceae	*Quercus geminata*	X	X
Fagales	Fagaceae	*Quercus hemisphaerica*		X
Fagales	Fagaceae	*Quercus laurifolia*	X	X
Fagales	Fagaceae	*Quercus marilandica*	X	
Fagales	Fagaceae	*Quercus minima*	X	
Fagales	Fagaceae	*Quercus myrtifolia*	X	X
Fagales	Fagaceae	*Quercus nigra*	X	X
Fagales	Fagaceae	*Quercus pumila*	X	
Fagales	Fagaceae	*Quercus virginiana*	X	X
Gentianales	Gentianaceae	*Sabatia brevifolia*	X	
Gentianales	Gentianaceae	*Sabatia calycina*	X	
Gentianales	Gentianaceae	*Sabatia grandiflora*		X
Gentianales	Gentianaceae	*Sabatia stellaris*	X	
Geraniales	Geraniaceae	*Geranium carolinianum*	X	
Rosales	Grossulariaceae	*Itea virginica*		X
Liliales	Haemodoraceae	*Lachnanthes caroliana*	X	X
Haloragales	Haloragaceae	*Proserpinaca palustris*		X
Haloragales	Haloragaceae	*Proserpinaca pectinata*	X	
Hamamelidales	Hamamelidaceae	*Hamamelis virginiana*	X	X
Hamamelidales	Hamamelidaceae	*Liquidambar styraciflua*	X	X
Hydrocharitales	Hydrocharitaceae	*Limnobium spongia*	X	
Illiciales	Illiciaceae	*Illicium parviflorum*	X	
Liliales	Iridaceae	*Calydorea coelestina*	X	
Liliales	Iridaceae	*Hypoxis curtissii*	X	
Liliales	Iridaceae	*Iris hexagona*	X	
Liliales	Iridaceae	*Sisyrinchium angustifolium*	X	
Liliales	Iridaceae	*Sisyrinchium atlanticum*	X	
Liliales	Iridaceae	*Sisyrinchium rosulatum*	X	
Juglandales	Juglandaceae	*Carya glabra*	X	X
Juncales	Juncaceae	*Juncus acuminatus*	X	
Juncales	Juncaceae	*Juncus coriaceus*	X	
Juncales	Juncaceae	*Juncus dichotomus*	X	
Juncales	Juncaceae	*Juncus effusus*	X	
Juncales	Juncaceae	*Juncus elliottii*	X	
Juncales	Juncaceae	*Juncus marginatus*	X	
Juncales	Juncaceae	*Juncus megacephalus*	X	
Juncales	Juncaceae	*Juncus polycephalus*	X	
Juncales	Juncaceae	*Juncus roemerianus*	X	
Juncales	Juncaceae	*Juncus scirpoides*	X	
Lamiales	Lamiaceae	*Hyptis mutabilis*	X	
Lamiales	Lamiaceae	*Lycopus americanus*	X	
Lamiales	Lamiaceae	*Mentha suaveolens*	X	
Lamiales	Lamiaceae	*Monarda punctata*	X	

Order	Family	Species	NPSpecies	This Study
Lamiales	Lamiaceae	*Physostegia purpurea*	X	
Lamiales	Lamiaceae	*Piloblephis rigida*	X	
Lamiales	Lamiaceae	*Salvia coccinea*	X	
Lamiales	Lamiaceae	*Salvia lyrata*	X	
Lamiales	Lamiaceae	*Scutellaria integrifolia*	X	
Lamiales	Lamiaceae	*Stachys floridana*	X	
Lamiales	Lamiaceae	*Teucrium canadense*	X	
Lamiales	Lamiaceae	*Trichostema dichotomum*	X	
Laurales	Lauraceae	*Cinnamomum camphora*	X	X
Laurales	Lauraceae	*Persea americana*	X	
Laurales	Lauraceae	*Persea borbonia*	X	X
Laurales	Lauraceae	*Persea palustris*	X	X
Arales	Lemnaceae	*Landoltia punctata*	X	
Arales	Lemnaceae	*Lemna aequinoctialis*	X	
Arales	Lemnaceae	*Lemna minor*		X
Arales	Lemnaceae	*Spirodela punctata*	X	
Scrophulariales	Lentibulariaceae	*Pinguicula caerulea*	X	
Scrophulariales	Lentibulariaceae	*Pinguicula pumila*	X	
Scrophulariales	Lentibulariaceae	*Utricularia subulata*	X	
Liliales	Liliaceae	*Aletris lutea*	X	
Liliales	Liliaceae	*Allium canadense var. canadense*	X	
Liliales	Liliaceae	*Asparagus aethiopicus*	X	
Liliales	Liliaceae	*Crinum asiaticum*	X	
Liliales	Liliaceae	*Nothoscordum bivalve*	X	
Liliales	Liliaceae	*Zigadenus densus*	X	
Linales	Linaceae	*Linum medium*	X	
Gentianales	Loganiaceae	*Gelsemium sempervirens*	X	X
Lycopodiales	Lycopodiaceae	*Lycopodiella alopecuroides*	X	
Lycopodiales	Lycopodiaceae	*Lycopodiella cernua var. cernua*	X	
Lycopodiales	Lycopodiaceae	*Lycopodiella prostrata*	X	
Polypodiales	Lygodiaceae	*Lygodium japonicum*	X	
Myrtales	Lythraceae	*Lagerstroemia indica*	X	
Magnoliales	Magnoliaceae	*Magnolia grandiflora*	X	X
Magnoliales	Magnoliaceae	*Magnolia virginiana*	X	X
Malvales	Malvaceae	*Gossypium barbadense*	X	
Malvales	Malvaceae	*Kosteletzkya virginica*	X	
Malvales	Malvaceae	*Malvaviscus arboreus*	X	
Malvales	Malvaceae	*Sida acuta*	X	
Malvales	Malvaceae	*Sida rhombifolia*	X	
Myrtales	Melastomataceae	*Rhexia alifanus*	X	
Myrtales	Melastomataceae	*Rhexia lutea*	X	
Myrtales	Melastomataceae	*Rhexia mariana*	X	
Myrtales	Melastomataceae	*Rhexia nashii*	X	
Myrtales	Melastomataceae	*Rhexia petiolata*	X	
Sapindales	Meliaceae	*Melia azedarach*	X	
Ranunculales	Menispermaceae	*Cocculus carolinus*	X	
Solanales	Menyanthaceae	*Nymphoides aquatica*		X
Ericales	Monotropaceae	*Monotropa uniflora*	X	
Urticales	Moraceae	*Fatoua villosa*	X	
Urticales	Moraceae	*Ficus pumila*	X	
Urticales	Moraceae	*Morus rubra*	X	X

Order	Family	Species	NPSpecies	This Study
Myricales	Myricaceae	*Morella caroliniensis*		X
Myricales	Myricaceae	*Morella cerifera*	X	X
Primulales	Myrsinaceae	*Ardisia crenata*	X	
Caryophyllales	Nyctaginaceae	*Boerhavia diffusa*	X	
Nymphaeales	Nymphaeaceae	*Nymphaea odorata*	X	
Cornales	Nyssaceae	*Nyssa sylvatica var. biflora*	X	X
Cornales	Nyssaceae	*Nyssa sylvatica var. sylvatica*	X	X
Santalales	Olacaceae	*Ximenia americana*	X	
Scrophulariales	Oleaceae	*Forestiera godfreyi*	X	
Scrophulariales	Oleaceae	*Forestiera segregata*	X	X
Scrophulariales	Oleaceae	*Fraxinus americana*	X	
Scrophulariales	Oleaceae	*Fraxinus caroliniana*	X	
Scrophulariales	Oleaceae	*Ligustrum japonicum*	X	
Scrophulariales	Oleaceae	*Osmanthus americanus*	X	X
Myrtales	Onagraceae	*Gaura angustifolia*	X	
Myrtales	Onagraceae	*Ludwigia linearis*	X	
Myrtales	Onagraceae	*Ludwigia linifolia*	X	
Myrtales	Onagraceae	*Ludwigia maritima*	X	
Myrtales	Onagraceae	*Ludwigia microcarpa*	X	
Myrtales	Onagraceae	*Ludwigia peruviana*	X	
Myrtales	Onagraceae	*Ludwigia pilosa*	X	
Myrtales	Onagraceae	*Ludwigia sphaerocarpa*	X	
Myrtales	Onagraceae	*Ludwigia suffruticosa*	X	
Myrtales	Onagraceae	*Ludwigia virgata*	X	
Myrtales	Onagraceae	*Oenothera fruticosa*	X	
Myrtales	Onagraceae	*Oenothera laciniata*	X	
Orchidales	Orchidaceae	*Corallorrhiza wisteriana*	X	
Orchidales	Orchidaceae	*Epidendrum conopseum*	X	
Orchidales	Orchidaceae	*Mesadenus polyanthus*	X	
Orchidales	Orchidaceae	*Platanthera ciliaris*	X	
Orchidales	Orchidaceae	*Spiranthes laciniata*	X	
Orchidales	Orchidaceae	*Spiranthes vernalis*	X	
Polypodiales	Osmundaceae	*Osmunda cinnamomea*	X	X
Polypodiales	Osmundaceae	*Osmunda regalis*	X	X
Geraniales	Oxalidaceae	*Oxalis corniculata*	X	
Geraniales	Oxalidaceae	*Oxalis rubra*	X	
Violales	Passifloraceae	*Passiflora incarnata*	X	X
Violales	Passifloraceae	*Passiflora lutea*	X	X
Caryophyllales	Phytolaccaceae	*Phytolacca americana*	X	X
Caryophyllales	Phytolaccaceae	*Phytolacca rigida*	X	
Caryophyllales	Phytolaccaceae	*Rivina humilis*	X	X
Pinales	Pinaceae	*Pinus elliottii*	X	X
Pinales	Pinaceae	*Pinus palustris*	X	X
Pinales	Pinaceae	*Pinus serotina*	X	X
Pinales	Pinaceae	*Pinus taeda*	X	X
Piperales	Piperaceae	*Peperomia humilis*	X	
Plantaginales	Plantaginaceae	*Plantago virginica*	X	
Hamamelidales	Platanaceae	*Platanus occidentalis*	X	
Plumbaginales	Plumbaginaceae	*Limonium carolinianum*	X	
Cyperales	Poaceae	*Agrostis hyemalis*	X	
Cyperales	Poaceae	*Andropogon elliottii*	X	

Table A-1. Continued

Order	Family	Species	NPSpecies	This Study
Cyperales	Poaceae	*Andropogon glomeratus var. glomeratus*	X	
Cyperales	Poaceae	*Andropogon glomeratus var. pumilus*	X	
Cyperales	Poaceae	*Andropogon virginicus var. glaucus*	X	X
Cyperales	Poaceae	*Andropogon virginicus var. virginicus*	X	X
Cyperales	Poaceae	*Aristida rhizomophora*	X	
Cyperales	Poaceae	*Aristida spiciformis*	X	
Cyperales	Poaceae	*Aristida stricta var. beyrichiana*	X	
Cyperales	Poaceae	*Arundinaria gigantea*	X	
Cyperales	Poaceae	*Bromus catharticus*	X	
Cyperales	Poaceae	*Calamovilfa curtissii*	X	
Cyperales	Poaceae	*Cenchrus gracillimus*	X	
Cyperales	Poaceae	*Cenchrus spinifex*	X	
Cyperales	Poaceae	*Chasmanthium laxum*	X	X
Cyperales	Poaceae	*Chasmanthium laxum ssp. sessiliflorum*	X	
Cyperales	Poaceae	*Chasmanthium laxum var. sessiliflorum*	X	
Cyperales	Poaceae	*Chasmanthium sessiliflorum*	X	
Cyperales	Poaceae	*Cynodon dactylon*		X
Cyperales	Poaceae	*Dactyloctenium aegyptium*	X	
Cyperales	Poaceae	*Dichanthelium aciculare*	X	
Cyperales	Poaceae	*Dichanthelium commutatum*	X	
Cyperales	Poaceae	*Dichanthelium laxiflorum*	X	
Cyperales	Poaceae	*Digitaria ciliaris*	X	
Cyperales	Poaceae	*Distichlis spicata*	X	
Cyperales	Poaceae	*Eleusine indica*	X	
Cyperales	Poaceae	*Elymus virginicus*	X	
Cyperales	Poaceae	*Eragrostis elliottii*	X	
Cyperales	Poaceae	*Eremochloa ophiuroides*	X	
Cyperales	Poaceae	*Eustachys petraea*	X	X
Cyperales	Poaceae	*Melica mutica*	X	
Cyperales	Poaceae	*Muhlenbergia capillaris*	X	
Cyperales	Poaceae	*Oplismenus hirtellus*	X	X
Cyperales	Poaceae	*Panicum anceps*	X	
Cyperales	Poaceae	*Panicum hemitomon*	X	X
Cyperales	Poaceae	*Panicum verrucosum*	X	
Cyperales	Poaceae	*Panicum virgatum*	X	
Cyperales	Poaceae	*Paspalum notatum*	X	X
Cyperales	Poaceae	*Paspalum notatum var. notatum*	X	
Cyperales	Poaceae	*Paspalum notatum var. saurae*	X	
Cyperales	Poaceae	*Paspalum setaceum*	X	
Cyperales	Poaceae	*Paspalum urvillei*	X	
Cyperales	Poaceae	*Piptochaetium avenaceum*	X	
Cyperales	Poaceae	*Poa annua*	X	
Cyperales	Poaceae	*Polypogon monspeliensis*	X	
Cyperales	Poaceae	*Saccharum giganteum*	X	
Cyperales	Poaceae	*Sacciolepis striata*	X	
Cyperales	Poaceae	*Setaria parviflora*	X	
Cyperales	Poaceae	*Sorghastrum secundum*	X	
Cyperales	Poaceae	*Sorghum bicolor*	X	
Cyperales	Poaceae	*Spartina alterniflora*	X	
Cyperales	Poaceae	*Spartina bakeri*	X	
Cyperales	Poaceae	*Spartina patens*	X	

Order	Family	Species	NPSpecies	This Study
Cyperales	Poaceae	Sphenopholis obtusata	X	
Cyperales	Poaceae	Sporobolus indicus	X	
Cyperales	Poaceae	Sporobolus indicus var. indicus	X	
Cyperales	Poaceae	Sporobolus virginicus	X	X
Cyperales	Poaceae	Stenotaphrum secundatum	X	
Cyperales	Poaceae	Tridens flavus var. flavus	X	
Cyperales	Poaceae	Tripsacum dactyloides	X	
Cyperales	Poaceae	Vulpia myuros	X	
Pinales	Podocarpaceae	Podocarpus macrophyllus	X	
Solanales	Polemoniaceae	Phlox drummondii	X	
Polygalales	Polygalaceae	Polygala grandiflora	X	
Polygalales	Polygalaceae	Polygala lutea	X	X
Polygalales	Polygalaceae	Polygala nana	X	
Polygonales	Polygonaceae	Polygonum hirsutum	X	
Polygonales	Polygonaceae	Polygonum hydropiperoides	X	
Polygonales	Polygonaceae	Polygonum persicaria	X	
Polygonales	Polygonaceae	Polygonum punctatum	X	
Polygonales	Polygonaceae	Rumex hastatulus	X	
Polypodiales	Polypodiaceae	Pecluma plumula	X	
Polypodiales	Polypodiaceae	Phlebodium aureum	X	
Polypodiales	Polypodiaceae	Pleopeltis polypodioides	X	
Liliales	Pontederiaceae	Eichhornia crassipes	X	
Liliales	Pontederiaceae	Pontederia cordata	X	
Caryophyllales	Portulacaceae	Portulaca pilosa	X	
Psilotales	Psilotaceae	Psilotum nudum	X	
Polypodiales	Pteridaceae	Cheilanthes microphylla	X	
Ranunculales	Ranunculaceae	Clematis catesbyana	X	
Ranunculales	Ranunculaceae	Clematis virginiana	X	
Rhamnales	Rhamnaceae	Berchemia scandens	X	
Rhamnales	Rhamnaceae	Frangula caroliniana	X	
Rhamnales	Rhamnaceae	Sageretia minutiflora	X	
Rosales	Rosaceae	Agrimonia incisa	X	
Rosales	Rosaceae	Photinia pyrifolia	X	X
Rosales	Rosaceae	Prunus caroliniana	X	X
Rosales	Rosaceae	Prunus serotina	X	X
Rosales	Rosaceae	Prunus serotina var. serotina	X	
Rosales	Rosaceae	Prunus umbellata	X	
Rosales	Rosaceae	Rosa laevigata	X	
Rosales	Rosaceae	Rubus argutus	X	
Rosales	Rosaceae	Rubus cuneifolius	X	
Rosales	Rosaceae	Rubus trivialis	X	
Rubiales	Rubiaceae	Cephalanthus occidentalis	X	X
Rubiales	Rubiaceae	Chiococca alba	X	
Rubiales	Rubiaceae	Diodia teres	X	X
Rubiales	Rubiaceae	Diodia virginiana	X	
Rubiales	Rubiaceae	Galium hispidulum	X	
Rubiales	Rubiaceae	Galium tinctorium	X	
Rubiales	Rubiaceae	Houstonia procumbens	X	
Rubiales	Rubiaceae	Mitchella repens	X	X
Rubiales	Rubiaceae	Oldenlandia corymbosa	X	
Rubiales	Rubiaceae	Oldenlandia uniflora	X	

Order	Family	Species	NPSpecies	This Study
Rubiales	Rubiaceae	*Psychotria nervosa*	X	
Rubiales	Rubiaceae	*Richardia brasiliensis*	X	X
Alismatales	Ruppiaceae	*Ruppia maritima*	X	
Sapindales	Rutaceae	*Citrus aurantium*	X	
Sapindales	Rutaceae	*Ptelea trifoliata*	X	X
Sapindales	Rutaceae	*Zanthoxylum clava-herculis*	X	
Salicales	Salicaceae	*Salix caroliniana*	X	
Hydropteridales	Salviniaceae	*Salvinia minima*	X	
Sapindales	Sapindaceae	*Sapindus marginatus*	X	
Sapindales	Sapindaceae	*Sapindus saponaria*	X	
Ebenales	Sapotaceae	*Sideroxylon alachuense*	X	
Ebenales	Sapotaceae	*Sideroxylon lycioides*		X
Ebenales	Sapotaceae	*Sideroxylon tenax*	X	X
Nepenthales	Sarraceniaceae	*Sarracenia minor*	X	
Piperales	Saururaceae	*Saururus cernuus*	X	
Scrophulariales	Scrophulariaceae	*Agalinis maritima*	X	
Scrophulariales	Scrophulariaceae	*Agalinis setacea*	X	
Scrophulariales	Scrophulariaceae	*Bacopa monnieri*	X	
Scrophulariales	Scrophulariaceae	*Buchnera americana*	X	
Scrophulariales	Scrophulariaceae	*Gratiola hispida*	X	
Scrophulariales	Scrophulariaceae	*Gratiola pilosa*	X	
Scrophulariales	Scrophulariaceae	*Gratiola ramosa*	X	
Scrophulariales	Scrophulariaceae	*Lindernia crustacea*	X	
Scrophulariales	Scrophulariaceae	*Nuttallanthus canadensis*	X	
Scrophulariales	Scrophulariaceae	*Schwalbea americana*	X	
Scrophulariales	Scrophulariaceae	*Scoparia dulcis*	X	
Scrophulariales	Scrophulariaceae	*Seymeria pectinata*	X	
Scrophulariales	Scrophulariaceae	*Veronica arvensis*	X	
Liliales	Smilacaceae	*Smilax auriculata*	X	X
Liliales	Smilacaceae	*Smilax bona-nox*	X	X
Liliales	Smilacaceae	*Smilax glauca*	X	X
Liliales	Smilacaceae	*Smilax laurifolia*	X	X
Liliales	Smilacaceae	*Smilax pumila*	X	X
Liliales	Smilacaceae	*Smilax rotundifolia*	X	
Liliales	Smilacaceae	*Smilax tamnoides*	X	
Solanales	Solanaceae	*Lycium carolinianum*	X	
Solanales	Solanaceae	*Physalis walteri*	X	
Solanales	Solanaceae	*Solanum americanum*	X	
Ebenales	Symplocaceae	*Symplocos tinctoria*	X	X
Pinales	Taxodiaceae	*Taxodium ascendens*		X
Theales	Theaceae	*Gordonia lasianthus*	X	X
Polypodiales	Thelypteridaceae	*Thelypteris kunthii*	X	
Typhales	Typhaceae	*Typha latifolia*	X	
Urticales	Ulmaceae	*Celtis laevigata*	X	X
Urticales	Ulmaceae	*Ulmus alata*	X	
Urticales	Ulmaceae	*Ulmus americana*	X	
Urticales	Urticaceae	*Boehmeria cylindrica*	X	
Urticales	Urticaceae	*Parietaria praetermissa*	X	
Urticales	Urticaceae	*Pilea microphylla*	X	
Lamiales	Verbenaceae	*Callicarpa americana*	X	X
Lamiales	Verbenaceae	*Lantana camara*	X	

Table A-1. Continued

Order	Family	Species	NPSpecies	This Study
Lamiales	Verbenaceae	*Lantana depressa*	X	
Lamiales	Verbenaceae	*Lantana depressa var. floridana*	X	
Lamiales	Verbenaceae	*Lantana montevidensis*	X	
Lamiales	Verbenaceae	*Phyla nodiflora*	X	
Lamiales	Verbenaceae	*Verbena brasiliensis*	X	
Violales	Violaceae	*Viola affinis*	X	
Violales	Violaceae	*Viola lanceolata*	X	
Violales	Violaceae	*Viola palmata*	X	
Violales	Violaceae	*Viola septemloba*	X	
Violales	Violaceae	*Viola sororia*	X	
Santalales	Viscaceae	*Phoradendron leucarpum*	X	
Rhamnales	Vitaceae	*Ampelopsis arborea*	X	
Rhamnales	Vitaceae	*Cissus trifoliata*	X	
Rhamnales	Vitaceae	*Parthenocissus quinquefolia*	X	X
Rhamnales	Vitaceae	*Vitis aestivalis*	X	X
Rhamnales	Vitaceae	*Vitis rotundifolia*	X	X
Commelinales	Xyridaceae	*Xyris ambigua*	X	
Commelinales	Xyridaceae	*Xyris jupicai*	X	
Commelinales	Xyridaceae	*Xyris platylepis*	X	

www.ingramcontent.com/pod-product-compliance
Lightning Source LLC
Chambersburg PA
CBHW080912290526
45795CB00007BA/2508